THE
CHIHUAHUA

ANNA KATHERINE NICHOLAS

Title page photo: Ch. Call's Delightful Design, #1 Chihuahua 1981 and 1982, all systems. Six all-breed Bests in Show; five Specialty Bests in Show; 22 times Group 1st; 47 additional Group placements. Selected by the Chihuahua Club of America as the "ideal Smoothcoat Chihuahua" to represent the breed in the A.K.C. Chihuahua Standard. Bred, owned, and handled by Annie D. Call, Kayside, Utah.

Distributed in the UNITED STATES by T.F.H. Publications, Inc., One T.F.H. Plaza, Neptune City, NJ 07753; in CANADA to the Pet Trade by H & L Pet Supplies Inc., 27 Kingston Crescent, Kitchener, Ontario N2B 2T6; Rolf C. Hagen Ltd., 3225 Sartelon Street, Montreal 382 Quebec; in CANADA to the Book Trade by Macmillan of Canada (A Division of Canada Publishing Corporation), 164 Commander Boulevard, Agincourt, Ontario M1S 3C7; in ENGLAND by T.F.H. Publications Limited, Cliveden House/Priors Way/Bray, Maidenhead, Berkshire SL6 2HP, England; in AUSTRALIA AND THE SOUTH PACIFIC by T.F.H. (Australia) Pty. Ltd., Box 149, Brookvale 2100 N.S.W., Australia; in NEW ZEALAND by Ross Haines & Son, Ltd., 18 Monmouth Street, Grey Lynn, Auckland 2, New Zealand; in SINGAPORE AND MALAYSIA by MPH Distributors (S) Pte., Ltd., 601 Sims Drive, #03/07/21, Singapore 1438; in the PHILIPPINES by Bio-Research, 5 Lippay Street, San Lorenzo Village, Makati Rizal; in SOUTH AFRICA by Multipet Pty. Ltd., 30 Turners Avenue, Durban 4001. Published by T.F.H. Publications, Inc. Manufactured in the United States of America by T.F.H. Publications, Inc.

Dedicated to the Chihuahua

A most wonderful breed of big-little dogs bringing joy and pleasure to the thousands of fortunate people who enjoy the companionship of one or more of them.

Contents

About the Author

Since early childhood, Anna Katherine Nicholas has been involved with dogs. Her first pets were a Boston Terrier, an Airedale, and a German Shepherd Dog. Then, in 1925, came the first of the Pekingese, a gift from a friend who raised them. Now her home is shared with two Miniature Poodles and numerous Beagles.

Miss Nicholas is best known throughout the Dog Fancy as a writer and as a judge. Her first magazine article, published in *Dog News* magazine around 1930, was about Pekingese, and this was followed by a widely acclaimed breed column, "Peeking at the Pekingese," which appeared for at least two decades, originally in *Dogdom*, then, following the demise of that publication, in *Popular Dogs*. During the 1940s she was a Boxer columnist for *Pure-Bred Dogs/American Kennel Gazette* and for *Boxer Briefs*. More recently many of her articles, geared to interest fanciers of every breed, have appeared in *Popular Dogs, Pure-Bred Dogs/American Kennel Gazette, Show Dogs, Dog Fancy, The World of the Working Dog*, and for both the Canadian publications, *The Dog Fancier* and *Dogs in Canada*. Her *Dog World* column, "Here, There and Everywhere," was the Dog Writers' Association of America winner of the Best Series in a Dog Magazine Award for 1979. Another feature article of hers, "Faster Is Not Better," published in *Canine Chronicle*, received Honorable Mention on another occasion.

In 1970 Miss Nicholas won the Dog Writers' Association Award for the Best Technical Book of the Year with her *Nicholas Guide to Dog Judging*. In 1979 the revision of this book again won this award, the first time ever that a revision has been so honored by this organization. Other important dog writer awards which Miss Nicholas has gained over the years have been the Gaines "Fido" and the *Kennel Review* "Winkies," these both on two occasions and each in the Dog Writer of the Year category.

It was during the 1930s that Miss Nicholas's first book, *The Pekingese*, appeared in print, published by the Judy Publishing Company. This book, and its second edition, sold out quickly and is now a collector's item, as is *The Skye Terrier Book* which was published during the 1960s by the Skye Terrier Club of America.

During recent years, Miss Nicholas has been writing books consistently for T.F.H. These include *Successful Dog Show Exhibiting, The Book of the Rottweiler, The Book of the Poodle, The Book of the Labrador Retriever, The Book of the English Springer Spaniel, The Book of the Golden Retriever, The Book of the German Shepherd Dog, The Book of the Shetland Sheepdog, The Book of the Miniature Schnauzer, The World of Doberman Pinschers,* and *The World of Rottweilers*. Plus, in the newest T.F.H. series, *The Maltese, The Keeshond, The Chow Chow, The Poodle, The Boxer, The Beagle, The Basset Hound, The Dachshund* (the latter three co-authored with Marcia A. Foy), *The German Pointer, The Collie, The Weimaraner, The Great Dane, The Dalmatian,* and numerous other titles. In the KW series she has done *Rottweilers, Weimaraners,* and *Norwegian Elkhounds*. And she has written American chapters for two popular English books purchased and published in the United States by T.F.H., *The Staffordshire Bull Terrier* and *The Jack Russell Terrier*.

Miss Nicholas's association with T.F.H. began in the early 1970s when she co-authored for them five books with Joan Brearley. These are *The Wonderful World of Beagles and Beagling* (also honored by the Dog Writers Association), *This is the Bichon Frise, The Book of the Pekingese, The Book of the Boxer,* and *This is the Skye Terrier*.

Since 1934 Miss Nicholas has been a popular dog show judge, officiating at prestigious events throughout the United States and Canada. She is presently approved for all Hounds, all Terriers, all

Ch. Farriston Wee Primrose at the Chihuahua Club of Greater New York Specialty, 1960. Mrs. Farris owner-handling. The author judging.

Toys and all Non-Sporting; plus all Pointers, English and Gordon Setters, Vizslas, Weimaraners, and Wirehaired Pointing Griffons in the Sporting Group and Boxers and Dobermans in Working. In 1970 she became only the third woman ever to have judged Best in Show at the famous Westminster Kennel Club event at Madison Square Garden in New York City, where she has officiated as well on some sixteen other occasions over the years. She has also officiated at such events as Santa Barbara, Chicago International, Morris and Essex, Trenton, Westchester, etc., in the United States; the Sportsman's and the Metropolitan among numerous others in Canada; and Specialty shows in several dozen breeds in both countries. She has judged in almost every one of the United States and in four of the Canadian Provinces. Her dislike of air travel has caused her to refrain from acceptance of the constant invitations to officiate in other parts of the world.

Ch. Tiny Mite's El Pepita, by Tiny Mite's Amber Gem ex Tiny Mite's Estrellita, the first homebred champion owned by the Robert L. DeJonges of Zeeland, Michigan. "Peppy" and his half brother, Ch. B-Beg's Mitee Koko, are both behind the homebred Long Coat line. Tiny Mite Chihuahuas are noted for the quality of their Long Coats as well as some outstanding Smooths.

Chapter 1

Origin of the Chihuahua

Of all the breeds of dog around the world, the Chihuahuas are the smallest. The history of the Chihuahua I have found to be the most intriguing of all those I have researched over the past few years. There are many variations and many theories to be found, some of which are generally accepted with credibility while others are looked upon with doubt.

It seems quite definitely agreed that the Chihuahua had its beginning in Mexico and in Central America. Two unique things about it are that it is a *true* Toy breed of tiny dogs which have been that way since the first of them was discovered. Thus they are not bred down from a combination of other breeds to reduce size. The question has arisen over whether or not they were actually discovered in Mexico and Central America, or whether they may have been brought there by the Spanish invaders. The believers of the former view point to the fact that archeologists have found that these tiny dogs were of the ancient culture of the Mayans, Toltecs and Aztecs, and that their remains have been found in Yucatan; and that they were important religious symbols of that period and area. In support of this we have read that the "tiny dog-like animals" were native to the Southwestern portion of North America, to Northern South America, to Panama, and known on the island of Cuba as long ago as the earliest recording of history.

The disbelievers brush this school of thought aside, claiming that Chihuahuas were brought to Mexico a century or so ago by the Chinese who were breeding dogs for diminutiveness of size. Others state that the dogs were actually developed by the Aztecs, descended from dogs brought in by the Spanish conquerors. Still another theory has been advanced by British fanciers who claim that the breed comes originally from the Island of Malta in the Mediterranean.

It is said that in 1160 A.D., when the Aztecs started wending their way slowly northward, the lives of the Chihuahuas were closely associated with those of the Indians. We have heard that the Maryland Museum of Natural Science has the skull and other skeletal parts of a tiny dog whose body was buried, prior to excavation, in the river bank burial ground of a long-extinct Indian tribe, which is commonly believed to have been usual practice. Not so, we hear from another side, this one claiming that at least one archeologist has stated that *no* true dog remains ever have been found in Aztec graves. Yet we have heard, for as long as the breed has interested us, that it was the custom for the Aztecs to have their dogs buried with their own remains; that they had strong religious beliefs regarding these dogs and their powers to ward off evil, to the point that we have accepted the theory that blue-colored dogs were considered sacred by the Aztecs; and that the burning of a red dog with the body of its master would transfer the sins of the master to the dog. Another religious belief was that these little dogs could guide the human soul to its eventual destination, taking it safely through the darkness of the underworld. How could any of this be possible—or the dogs even known there in those days—had the Chihuahuas not existed in Aztec territory *prior* to the arrival of the Spanish conquerors?

Ancestors of the Chihuahua are highly praised as pets, and were extremely popular as such with the Toltecs in their days of wealth. We recall reading at one time that along with their religious symbolism, they were also supposed to possess outstanding curative powers, frequently being used as close companions to the sick or elderly under the theory that the proximity of the dog's body to that of the master could draw the illness from the human being to the dog.

A heavy balance of evidence points to the Chihuahua as being truly a product of the Western Hemisphere, named for the state of Chihuahua and known in Mexico as the Chihuahueno. There is a legend that Chihuahuas once ran wild throughout parts of Mexico, although numerous Mexican expeditions have been unable to discover any basis for this tale. From the point of view of common sense, it would seem unlikely that dogs as tiny as these could have survived this type of living; but then, one never knows.

Another speculative point in Chihuahua history is that involving "which came first, the Long Coat or the Smooth." One theory is that the original dogs were the Long Coats, but that they did not attract the public eye until after the Smooths had outnumbered them. The explanation for the latter concept is that the hot climate, combined with centuries of interbreeding, would have led to reduced size and vitality and gradual loss of coat, which applies to the Smooth Coats as compared to these earlier Long Coats which were larger and more robust than the Smooths, as well as more heavily coated. It is further speculated that early breeders may have introduced other Toy dogs of heavier coat to bring back the Long Coats of the early "Shepherd Chihuahua," which was the name by which that variety was called in early times. This gives rise to indignant voices saying this is to infer that the Long Coat Chihuahua is a mongrel, which is not the case. As an example, the Rough Coated and Smooth Collies are cited as both being accepted as Collies, which is also true that the Long Coat and Smooth Chihuahuas are equally pure in Chihuahua breeding.

Our modern Chihuahua is descended from the Techichi, a type of dog indigenous to Central America as long ago as the 9th century A.D. These dogs were owned by the Toltecs and their presence has been established as far back as several hundred years.

Thein's Maximilian II taking Best of Winners, Long Coat, at Westminster 1955. Mignon Murray, always a great Chihuahua fancier and breeder, now a popular and noted judge, is handling.

Chapter 2

Development in the United States

Those superlative little Chihuahuas we see in the show ring nowadays, their outstanding quality, and the exciting records they are making are a tribute, actually, not only to our current breeders and owners, but to the pioneer breeders who provided the excellent foundation stock on which to build present bloodlines. It is thanks to them that the breeders now producing such splendid dogs who are capable of consistent Best in Show wins, multiple Groups, and other outstanding achievements are enabled to do so successfully, for a building is only as strong as its foundation. Thus we pay tribute to the Chihuahua breeders of yesteryear as well as to those of the present time.

It has been recorded that James Watson, well-known authority on dogs, in 1888 brought one of the earliest Chihuahuas to the United States from Mexico. This would seem to have started the ball rolling toward Chihuahua popularity here, as we have read that not too much later the breed started attracting attention here as widely spread as from coast to coast, with particular emphasis along the Eastern seaboard (New York, New Jersey, and the Philadelphia area of Pennsylvania), in California along the Pacific, and in such parts of the Midwest as Illinois, Ohio, Kentucky, and

15

Lewis Ku Tee Girl, handled by Peggy Anspach Wolf to a win at Westchester K.C. under the author in 1958.

The author's Mother, Mrs. Gretchen M. Nicholas, judging a very consistently winning Smooth of the 1940s. Ch. Bedford's Gay Lady, owned and handled by Mrs. Bedford, won the Variety with ease at many eastern dog shows of that period.

Missouri. There are records of some having been shown at the dog shows of this period.

It was during the early 1900s that two Philadelphians visited Mexico where they purchased what was to become some of the earliest breeding stock of Chihuahuas in the United States. These were author Owen Wister, who wrote *The Virginian,* and Charles Stewart. These gentlemen selected carefully and brought back Chihuahuas who are credited with contributing well to the foundation of the breed in this country.

We have found reference to the first Chihuahua registered with the American Kennel Club as having been one named Midget, in the year 1904. By 1908 reportedly numerous Chihuahuas were registered and bred, by H. H. Edwards from Shawnee, Oklahoma, which later turned up owned by Frank R. Stephenson whose Shady Brook Kennels were located at Bound Brook, New Jersey. These, too, were Mexican imports and helped to create our modern American-bred Chihuahua. Little, I am sure, did these pioneer breeders and importers envision the growth in popularity the breed they had helped to introduce here would achieve; nor that less than a hundred years later this would have become one of the most popular breeds in America, with the annual number of registrations rising to the point where today the breed remains steadily among the most numerically well loved here!

The Chihuahua Club of America was founded in 1923 by a group of fanciers in the metropolitan New York area. These included Mrs. Henrietta Proctor Donnell (later Mrs. Reilly), Ida H. Garrett, Alice Dobbs, Rose Clark, and M. R. Muller, the latter becoming the club's first president while Mrs. Garrett was the first to serve as its secretary. The club's initial Specialty Show was held on Saturday, May 19, 1928, in conjunction with the Queensboro Kennel Club all-breed event.

By the mid-1930s it had become apparent that perhaps, due to the widespread growing popularity of Chihuahuas in all sections of the country, the breed might be better served by an annual meeting and Specialty Show located more centrally, thus easier to attend by more members from more areas. Chicago being easily accessible from practically all parts of the United States seemed ideal, and, largely due to the efforts of Miss Helen Nowicki, long-time editor of the Chicago-based *Dog World* magazine, the Chihuahua Club of America moved its annual events there (a move we are sure has never been regretted), making that city its new and permanent headquarters—a very wise decision and choice as it has turned out. Helen Nowicki, incidentally, is thought of by a great many Toy breeders as a Pomeranian breeder, which is true, but Chihuahuas have been another of the breeds she has raised, loved, and worked for over the years.

In the beginning, the Chihuahua Club of America became part of the show-giving group known as the Western Specialty Clubs Association which banded together to share facilities and expenses for the staging of a number of breed Specialty Shows under one roof. Eventually it was decided that the Chihuahua folks wanted to "go it alone," but not until some 20 years later, during which time the success of the event had steadily been increasing. When the move was made, it was to various hotels in the Chicago area which continue to be the home base for these Specialties and annual meetings today.

In salute to the early winners, following are the names of the Chihuahuas and their owners who won Best of Breed at the Nationals held between 1935 and 1960 inclusive:

Champion Ai Si Ora Principe, Anna B. Vinyard, on two occasions

Champion Alegria Pinta, Mrs. Charles H. Willits

Don Juan Patro, Mayme Cole Holmes

Champion Phoenix Chico, Mrs. Henrietta Proctor Donnell Reilly

Champion Little Meron V, Ida H. Garrett

Don Juan Alfonso, Silvina Febles

Champion La Rey, Anna B. Vinyard

Pate's Tu La Rosa, Mrs. S. Poulsen

Meronette, Olive C. Grudier, on three occasions

Champion El Gusto Wakita, Mr. and Mrs. Newman K. Briggs

Champion La Oro Marinero, Anna B. Vinyard

Don Quixote Grudier, Olive C. Grudier

Champion La Oro Damisela, Anna B. Vinyard, on two occasions

Champion Carsello's La-Zorita, Nadine Carsello

Thurmer's Nita, Tressa E. Thurmer

Champion Thurmer's Staar Rusty, Monzell Staar

Champion Glavern Mona, Dr. C. L. Allen

Champion Ross's Bonita Bambino, Albert H. Ross

Champion Tejano Texas Kid, Mrs. Bob Roberts, on two occasions

Champion Bill's Black Bart, Thomas W. Jenkins

Champion Rowe's Wee Margo De Oro, Beatrice and Leslie Rowe

Champion Lanewood's Mister Bill, Mr. and Mrs. David O. Lane

Champion Teeny Wee's Kitten, Kathryn F. Lacher

Bill's Cotton Tammy, Thomas W. Jenkins

The foregoing list should give our readers a fair idea of the leading Chihuahuas and their owners during the important quarter century of breed development covered. You will find these dogs and these kennels appearing consistently behind current pedigrees, should you be among those who enjoy doing hereditary research on the Chihuahuas of our time.

Mrs. Donnell and Mrs. Garrett were the two earliest Chihuahua breeders of my personal acquaintance, having been located in my own home area in the years when I was first starting to judge the breed. Mrs. Donnell, (or Mrs. Reilly as she became for awhile then resumed the name Donnell) had a huge number of Chihuahuas at her Etty Haven Kennels, right along the shore of Long Island Sound at Larchmont, New York. She was devoted to the breed, although owner of several others, too, including Affenpinschers, Miniature Pinschers and Schipperkes; but one had the feeling that the Chihuahuas were most especially her favorites, although closely pressed by the Affenpinschers. She showed her own dogs, doing so very consistently at shows in the New York/New Jersey/New England areas.

The Chihuahua Club of America celebrated its Golden Anniversary in 1973. The annual Specialty that year drew 199 dogs in the then record entry of 292. A solid gold medallion was struck especially for this occasion; needless to say, these medals are highly prized collectors' items at this time!

Best of Breed at the Golden Anniversary Specialty was Champion Ervin's Frosty Snowman owned by Ronald D. and Ann B. Myers.

As was fast becoming an annual custom with the parent Specialty Clubs of many popular breeds, the Chihuahua Club of America decided during the mid-1970s to add an annual rotating spring Specialty Show to its schedule, thus enabling fanciers from around the country to enjoy a National Specialty in their own area, hosted by a local Specialty Club. The first such site chosen was Atlanta, Georgia, in 1977, where the Chihuahua Club of Atlanta was host to the National for a truly super-exciting Chihuahua occasion. For 1978 the invitation of the Chihuahua Club of Southern California was accepted, which made this the first time ever that a Chihuahua Club of America annual meeting took place west of the Mississippi River. Then, winding up the 1970s, the Dallas Chihuahua Club stepped into the picture as host to the rotating National there. These rotating Regionals have become firmly entrenched now in the year's Chihuahua activities, sharing honors each year with the traditional autumn Specialty in Chicago.

Of the early Chihuahua breeders, at least several deserve very special recognition for their accomplishments. One of these is Mrs. Harry S. Peaster from Philadelphia, whose La Rex Doll Kennels was among the earliest, famous for Toy Poodles and for Chihuahuas. Mrs. Peaster produced an imposing list of famous winning Chihuahuas in the 1930s-1940s period (by which time actually hers had long been a famous name in the Toy Fancy) and, best of all, her La Rex Doll champions provided foundation stock for many others. For instance, in the late 1930s we find a Westminster catalogue listing Mrs. Lloyd Reeves of Tattoo Kennels (primarily known for her famed Dalmatians although also a Chihuahua fancier then, who is still breeding today in Florida and in Vermont, between which places she now divides her time). Mrs. Reeves at that time was showing Champion Just Mona, daughter of Champion La Rex Doll Don Juan, and another bitch, Freckles, who was also by Don Juan ex La Papita of Miniature, bred by Mrs. Peaster. Mrs. Charles H. Willets's Champion Alegria Pinta, a National Specialty Best of Breed, was by El Toro of Alegria ex Champion La Rex Doll Hermosita. Mrs. Donnell had a daughter of Champion Coy La Rex Doll Chicula. Through the years, La Rex Doll stock has played a background role behind an amazing number of champions and bloodlines.

Mrs. Peaster's niece, Florence Clark Gamberg, was already started in her aunt's footsteps as a successful Chihuahua breeder back in those days, and has numerous champions to her own credit. More recently she became a Pug owner and is an extremely popular A.K.C.-approved judge, now living in Florida.

The Midwest seems to have been especially fortunate in its Chihuahua breeders, with some of the most famous having been situated in that part of the country. For example, Ohio was the "home territory" for Anna B. Vinyard and La Oro Kennels, a kennel which is truly a legend in the breed. Mrs. Vinyard's early

Famous Long Coat of the 1950s, Ch. Ross's Bonita Bambino, handled by the late Clara Alford to Best of Variety under the author, Westminster 1955.

success stories included Champion Ai Si Ora Principe, twice winner of Best of Breed at the National, and champion La Oro Damisela who also twice scored National Specialty Bests in Show as well as Champion La Rey, Champion La Oro Marinero, (both National Best in Show winners), Champion La Oro Perilla, Champion Mi Oro Don Meron, and Champion La Oro Muchacho to name just a few of the standard-bearers. Mrs. Vinyard's influence on the breed has been tremendous. We salute her with true admiration.

One of the other ladies who stands among the "greats" in the Chihuahua world is Olive C. Grudier from Columbus. Her fabulous dogs included Champion Meronette Grudier (Little Meron IV ex Pocahontas) who was three times winner of the National. Need we say more?

We find mention of Mrs. Clara Dobbs reaching all the way back to 1914 when she was photographed with a Chihuahua imported from Mexico, Peggy by name. Others we associate with this lady are the great Don Sergio; Champion Little Meron X; the earlier Champion Little Meron IV; Champion No No Amada Meron; and numerous others who bore the Meron identification.

Tressa Thurmer, now of Marco Island, Florida, is formerly from Illinois where her Chihuahuas earned considerable fame, widely admired for their special trademark—excellent, beautiful, and correctly typical heads. One of her most famous dogs was the Best in Show winning Champion Thurmer's Little Gayla, who was Top Chihuahua in America in 1964. There are numerous others on this lady's "success roster" as well, for her breeding was superb and her achievements outstanding.

On the Pacific Coast, an early breeder of renown was Mrs. Alma Rhodes whose dogs were famous in both the show ring and in obedience. Among the latter was Champion Rhodes La Cara, C.D.X.

Here in the East there were some very loyal and dedicated breeders making Chihuahua competition keen and exciting. Mrs.

A very famous historic Longcoat Chihuahua, Ch. Forest View's Lucky of Oz, with H. Wm Ohman, belonged to Oz Kennels, A. Mellinger, H. Wm. Ohman, and Richard Racheter, Matawan, New Jersey. Winning here on May 26, 1968, Mr. Ohman handling. This was the foundation dog from "Oz" and all dogs from this kennel descend from him.

This is the fabulous Ch. Tejano Texas Kid with his handler, the late Clara Alford, winning Best of Variety at Westminster in 1955 under the author. Texas Kid was owned by Merle Roberts. This stunning little dog had enormous impact on the shows and judges, racking up multiple Best in Show and Toy Group honors.

David Crouse produced some real "showstoppers" whom I recall with tremendous admiration. The Theins were long-time breeders who consistently produced winners, including Champion Thein's Little Man who was purchased by Mrs. Donnell. Mrs. Emma Haug was very much into this breed with a steady procession of really typey and beautiful Chihuahuas. Among hers were Champion Haug's Wee Chita Girl, a successful "special" for her owner at show after show with some Group placements, born in 1939 by Thein's Woolie Wood ex Thein's Louida. Champion Haug's Queen Victoria was a stunning little bitch, as was Champion Haug's Princess Donna Doll. Among her dogs, we especially liked Champion Haug's Wee King Pedro of Union and Champion Haug's Dapper Dan.

Mrs. R. A. Bedford was a highly successful exhibiting fancier with her lovely Smooth bitch, Champion Bedford's Gay Lady and with her homebred Champion Pate's Tu La Rosa. Gay Lady in particular won quite steadily in specials classes with an enthusiastic following of admirers among the judges.

Silvina Febles had numerous Chihuahuas which she herself showed or sold to show homes. Thelma Wolf had a Champion dog, Wolf's Dustin, by Champion Duke of Lange ex Mercay's Merrie Lady who won and sired winners. Dorothy B. Olenik, in the 1950s, joined the breeder-exhibitor ranks with sizeable entries, including her Champion Olenik's Little Red Robbin.

Who in the Chihuahua world is not familiar with the name Grace L. Shroyer? This dedicated lady, who we understand is partially of Indian heritage, has been in dogs since 1918, owning numerous breeds. When her enthusiastic interest turned to Chihuahuas, it was a fortunate day for the breed as this is another lady who has made important contributions to its progress. Mrs. Shroyer's breeding program has been credited with having produced and being in the background of some of the finest Long Coats this breed has ever known. Among her winners have been Champion Shroyer's Rock Robin, Best of Breed at the National Specialty in 1969; Champion Shroyer's Apache Rain Prince, Best of Breed at the National in 1975; Champion Shroyer's Coca Mia from the mid-1960s; Champion Shroyer's Ricky Robin; the Smooth Champion Prince Benji, Toy Group winner in the mid-1970s; Champion Shroyer's Half Penny, to name just a few.

On the following pages we bring you the stories of some of America's Chihuahua kennels which are currently active. We can think of no better way to describe the progress of a breed than by telling our readers of the individual breeders who are working for its continued success. We have selected a cross section of the United States, presenting some of the current leading winners and summarizing the background from which they have been produced.

A kennel name is important to a breeder, and the name should be selected and used from the time of one's first homebred litter. Kennel names are chosen in many different ways. Sometimes the name of the street on which the breeder is located is the choice; or the name is a form of one's own name or a coined combination of the names of family members. Often the kennel is named for a child who is especially enthusiastic about the dogs. Many use the name, or a combination of the names, of their foundation dogs (either their proper names or the call names of these dogs). Whatever strikes your fancy is appropriate, as long as the name does not have an excessive number of letters (remember that the number of letters in a dog's complete name is limited for registration purposes, and the kennel name is included in the count) and does not infringe on anyone's prior rights. Such a name will identify you and your Chihuahuas through future generations.

A kennel name can be registered with the American Kennel Club, thus becoming exclusively your own for a stated period of time. A kennel name thus registered may not be used by any other person when registering a dog with the American Kennel Club unless, in writing, you specifically permit another person to do so (as would be the case with a puppy you have sold). Information regarding the procedure is available from the American Kennel Club, 51 Madison Avenue, New York, N.Y. 10010. There are specific requirements regarding the type of name eligible for registration as your kennel name, and a fee is to be paid if one chooses this course.

To be of greatest value, kennel names should be applied to all dogs bred by your kennel, as then the dog and its background are immediately identified. A good way of registering each of your dogs is to start each name with your kennel title if the dog is a homebred and to end the dog's name with the addition of the kennel name if it is a dog you have purchased.

On the following pages we pay tribute to some of our long-time breeders and some of the newer ones. On the shoulders of the latter squarely rests the task of carrying on and preserving what has been accomplished and the responsibility for the future well being of the Chihuahua breed.

Ch. Dartan's Pirate Blackbeard, by Ch. Handwerk's Pirate Blackbeard ex Dartan's Black Eyed Susan, owned by Jean and Russ Kruetzman, Jo-El Kennels, Creve Coeur, Missouri. Best in Specialty Show of the Chihuahua Club of America 1984 in an entry of 275. #2 Top Producer in 1984. #3 ranked Smooth Coat in 1984.

Chapter 3

Some Well-Known Chihuahua Kennels in the United States

BAYARD

Bayard Chihuahuas, Cambridge, Maryland, are owned by Melanie Newall and include some very well-known members of the breed.

Pride of place at this kennel would seem to go to the elegant Long Coat Champion RJR Reginald of Bayard, who was bred by RJR Kennels. Reginald is the sire of 20 champions as of September 1985, and has himself enjoyed a highly successful show career as well.

Reginald's wins include Best of Variety at the Chihuahua Club of Atlanta, at the Chihuahua Club of New York, and at the Chihuahua Club of Maryland, plus Best Stud Dog in Show for three consecutive years at the Chihuahua Club of America. He has many additional Bests of Variety to his credit, along with numerous Group placements. All in all, he is an extremely worthy representative of his breed.

Champion Bayard Alvin of Reginald RJR is a son of Reginald ex Champion RJR Feathers Gold of Bayard. Alvin, as a puppy,

Ch. Brite Star Christmas Canis, C.D., High in Trial winner, 198.5 score. Finished championship with three majors. Ranked #1 Obedience Chihuahua 1984. Ranked in Top Ten All- Breed Obedience Toys in 1984. GKCDTC Perpetual Trophy winner in all-breed competition for highest score average of dog going for a title during 1984. Owned by Brite Star Chihuahuas, Ms. Elizabeth Bickel.

was Best Puppy in Sweepstakes, Best Bred-by Exhibitor in Show, and Best of Winners at the Chihuahua Club of America Specialty in Chicago, and Best of Variety at the Chihuahua Club of New York. He is the sire of eight champions.

Others of note from this kennel include Champion Bayard Tinkerbelle of Alvin who was Reserve Winners Bitch at the Chihuahua Club of Michigan Specialty in 1982, Champion Bayard Raw Silk of Reginald, and the current "young hopeful" of the family at the time of writing, Champion Bayard Belle of the Ball, by Reginald ex I Love Lucy, Best of Winners and Best of Opposite Sex at the Chihuahua Club of America in 1985. Melanie Newall can indeed take pride in her success as a breeder and in the splendid quality of her homebreds.

BRITE STAR

Brite Star Chihuahuas are owned by Ms. Elizabeth Bickel and are located at Kansas City, Missouri. This is a fairly young kennel, having been started in 1977. Despite the youth of both the kennel and its charming young owner, they like to think of themselves as an integral part of the future of the breed. During the past few years, countless Brite Star homebreds have been Specialty Show winners; many have gained their titles in both show and obedience competition, and numerous others are well on the way to following suit.

Ms. Bickel's foundation bitch is Brite Star Polaris of Shroyer, and the bloodlines with which she works are predominantly Shroyer and some Dartan tracing back to Shroyer. Another foundation bitch is the lovely black Glaisdaleast Fantasia, C.D., imported from England and primarily of Rozavel bloodlines, who became the first obedience Chihuahua at Brite Star Kennels. She arrived at Brite Star in 1978. At her first show, the Chihuahua Club of America weekend in Dallas, at age eight months, Fantasia went Reserve plus a good win in the Sweepstakes. She then broke her leg, necessitating immediate retirement from the ring. Fantasia's bloodlines run through all of the current Brite Star champions through her only son, Brite Star Apollo, C.D.

Ms. Bickel currently is showing her fifth generation Brite Star homebred puppies, taking great pride in each generation of them.

A favorite Long Coat at Brite Star is Champion Brite Star Little Dipper. Starting out with a five-point Specialty major he immediately obtained two more similar victories at his next shows, again out of puppy classes, by going Best of Variety over Group-placing specials. An active young stud, he is also a well-mannered house pet, personality plus, and his owner's ideal of a conformation Chihuahua.

Little Dipper's half-sister (and also his cousin), Champion Brite Star Galactic Magic, was Best of Opposite Sex to Best of Breed at the Chihuahua Club of Maryland on the only occasion she was ever specialed at time of writing.

Ms. Bickel does cross coats in her breeding program (i.e., interbreed the Smooths and the Long Coats), her feeling being that she gets excellent coats on both varieties by doing so. Although Longs predominate at Brite Star, both Little Dipper and Magic have Smooth sires and Long Coat dams. Magic's Specialty-winning little sister is a Long Coat. Now Magic has had a mixed coat litter sired by a Long Coat. Ms. Bickel comments, "It works for me."

With numerous Best Brood Bitch wins at Specialty Shows, Polaris was a Top Producer for 1981 with three Long Coat daughters, all breeder-owner-handled, finishing within three months. Her daughter, Champion Brite Star Milky Way, is proving equally successful at producing champions, and it looks as though Milky Way's daughter, Galactic Magic, may also. Ms. Bickel strongly believes that a show kennel is only as good as its bitches.

Besides notable success in the conformation ring, Brite Star Chihuahuas are rapidly becoming a legend in obedience, of which you will read later on in this book in that section devoted to our obedience Chihuahuas.

CALL'S

Call's Chihuahuas are owned by Chester P. and Annie D. Call of Kaysville, Utah. The Calls started their linebreeding of Chihuahuas with the acquisition of Call's Honeybun of Charmarie, whom they bred to Champion Brecon's Individualist, a Chihuahua whose type and quality especially appealed to them. Honeybun was by Amigo Kid of Charmarie ex Darling Beauty of Charmarie. Individualist was a son of Champion Barnell's Rick-O-Shay of Misalou ex Champion Marie's Wee Sheba. Individualist appears in current Call's pedigrees as often as half a dozen times; Honeybun at least several. These two had a tremendous influence on the quality and development of this splendid Chihuahua line.

Ch. Bayard I Love Lucy of Alvin, Longcoat daughter of Ch. Bayard Alvin of Reginald RJR ex Primavera's Lina of Bayard. Reserve Winners Bitch, Chihuahua Club of America 1982 at Tulsa, Oklahoma; Reserve Winners Bitch, Chihuahua Club of America 1982 in Chicago; Winners Bitch at the Chihuahua Club of Maryland. The dam of three champions, Lucy was bred and is owned by Melanie Newell, Cambridge, Maryland.

Call's Little Painted Parader taking Group 1st in an all-breed Match Show at just six months old. By Ch. Hutchen's 'N Humphrey Lil Cru ex Ch. Call's Little Tawnee Tutone. Bred, owned, and shown by Annie D. Call. Now a champion and the sire of the famous Ch. Call's Delightful Design.

Ch. Gindon Bo Jangles of Dartan winning an all-breed Best in Show at South Bend, Indiana, in June 1975, handled by James Lehman for owners Darwin and Tanya Delaney, Essexville, Michigan. Bred by Alice Page, by Ch. Dartan's Blaze Away of Gindon ex Bill's Red Rose, this famous and important little dog was also Best in Specialty Show at the Chihuahua Club of America National in 1974 and #1 Smooth Chihuahua Dog in the Nation in 1975.

Champion Call's Delightful Design began her show career at the age of seven months at the Chihuahua Club of Atlanta Specialty in April 1980 when the author of this book awarded her Reserve Winners from the 6-9 month puppy class after having earlier that day won the Sweepstakes. Since that time she has earned six Best in Show wins under judges Derek Rayne, Vincent Perry, J. D. Jones, Glen Sommers, Emil Klinckhardt, and Robert Caviness. Her picture was selected by the Chihuahua Club of America as the ideal Smooth Coat Chihuahua to be sent to the American Kennel Club to represent the Standard for the Breed. Delightful Design was #1 Chihuahua for the years 1981 and 1982. She has two Bests of Varieties at Specialty Shows and three Best of Breed wins at them, plus, in Variety Group competition, 22 times Group 1st; 17 times Group 2nd, and 15 times each Group 3rd and Group 4th. Always owner-handled, Annie Call notes with pride.

DARTAN

Darwin Delaney purchased his first pair of registered Chihuahuas in 1952, and already had a small kennel when he married Tanya in 1957. Dartan Chihuahuas, at Essexville, Michigan, are a combination of the Delaneys' two names, DARwin and TANya, and they have become very famous and widely admired in their breed and in the dog show world generally.

The majority of the early Dartan dogs carried some La Oro, Don Apache, and Miniatura bloodlines. Later Missalou, Shroyer, Luce, and Bills were added. The Delaneys constantly are on the lookout for a dog or a bitch with qualities that will add to their bloodlines.

The first from this kennel to gain championship was the home-bred Champion Dartan's Lucky Strike in 1962. Since then over 100 quality Chihuahuas have gained title under the Dartan name, most of them owner-handled.

There have been numerous outstanding Dartan dogs over the years. To mention a few of them, and their accomplishments, let's start with Champion Dartan's Creme De Co Co Shroyer, who was #1 Long Coat in 1965 when very few of this Variety (or any Chihuahuas at all) were placing in Toy Groups.

Then there was Champion Gindon Bo Jangles of Dartan, the Delaneys' first All Breed Best in Show winner who made the breakthrough to that honor in June 1975 at South Bend, Indiana, under judge Haskell Schuffman, handled by James Lehman. Jangles was also Best of Breed at the Chihuahua Club of America National Specialty in 1974 and #1 Smooth dog in 1975. His daughter, Champion Bo Jangles Charisma of Dartan, was #1 Smooth bitch in 1977, and Best of Breed at the Chihuahua Club of America National Specialty in 1976. Champion Dartan Dominique D'Quachitah was all-breed Best in Show on July 25, 1981 at Waukesha, Wisconsin, under Mrs. Jane Kay, owned at that time by Linda George, now at home again with her breeders, the Delaneys.

The Delaneys comment that, "Although we enjoy exhibiting and winning with our dogs, our greatest joy is in breeding and producing Chihuahuas of truly good quality in an effort to improve the breed and raise their esteem in the eyes of others. For this reason we are most proud of our Top Producers, the sires and dams of our famous winners."

Champion Handwerk's Lucky Strike was the Top Producing Chihuahua Sire for 1982 with eight champion offspring that year. His champions to date total 17, two of whom are themselves Top Producers: Champion Dartan's Pirate Blackbeard and Champion Dartan's Elfin Magic. Lucky is also the sire of Champion Ehl's Mighty Lunar of Dartan, a seven-time all-breed Best in Show winner.

Champion Dartan's Super Dude, Top Producing sire for 1981 with six champions that year, has produced a total of 14 champions to the present time. These include Champion Dartan's Calamity Jane, dam of all-breed Best in Show winner Champion Dartan Dominique D'Quachitah and Champion Dartan's Bristol Cream, winner of many Group placements and Specialty Bests of Breed.

Champion Dartan's Pirate Blackbeard, Top Producing sire for 1984 with seven champions that year, has now produced 12 champions, eight of whom are multiple Group placers, and who include Champion Jo-El's Drummer Boy, all-breed Best in Show winner. Pirate has multiple Group placements of his own, plus Best of Breed at the 1984 Chihuahua Club of America Specialty where he defeated the Club's largest entry to date, 277 dogs. At the time of this exciting occasion, Pirate was owned by Joan and Russ Kruetzman and handled by Terri Lydden. He, too, is now home again with his breeders at Dartan.

Champion Dartan's Elfin Magic has already produced 17 champions, among them Champion Quachitah For Your Eyes Only, a four-time all-breed Best in Show winner who was the first Chihuahua ever to win a Group 1st at the Westminster Kennel Club Dog Show.

Dartan's Connie not only was Top Producing Chihuahua Dam for 1984, but was, as well, Top Producing Dam among all of the Toy breeds that year with five champion offspring. Connie's total to date is nine champions, including Champion Dartan's Constant Comment with 19 Group placements and Champion Dartan's Saree So Sweet who finished owner-handled with two Group 1sts from the classes.

The latest star as we write is Champion Dartan's Tailor Made, who on his first show weekend, when just six months old, won two 5-point majors, Best of Variety over specials, and a Group 2nd. Tailor is another owner-handled homebred.

FLINT'S

Flint's Chihuahuas, at Dayton, Ohio, are owned by Robert L. and Patsy Sue Flint. This kennel, which has bred Best in Show winners, is the home of many champions in both the Long Coat and Smooth Coat varieties. The Flints have never raised any other breed, and intend never to do so as they are completely happy with their own.

The Flints' Chihuahuas are descended from such illustrious stars as great Champion Tejano Texas Kid, for many years the Top Winning Chihuahua of All Time; International Champion Jay's Speedy Gonzalas, Champion Shroyer's Rickee Robin, and Champion Ells Mighty Lunar of Dartan.

The Flints produced or owned or finished 28 champions within a ten-year period. Among them is Champion Flint's Lil Lucky Robin, the history making world renowned *first* and to date *only Long Coat male* Chihuahua in the United States to have gained an all-breed Best in Show in the United States. Lucky was Top Producing Sire for 1980, the Top Producing Dam that year having been the Flints' Champion Flint's Lil Love Robin.

Champion Flint's Carbon Copy was #3 Long Coat 1982 Kennel Review System, having won 83 Bests of Variety, including eight Specialty Bests of Variety and two Specialty Bests in Show, plus

Ch. Flint's Lucky Jeri Robin, by Ch. Shroyers Jeri Robin ex Flint's Happy Go Lucky Girl, was bred and is owned by Robert and Patsy Flint, handled by Jim Lehman. Here taking points at Dayton 1979.

The Flints are constantly striving in their breeding program for quality Chihuahuas. They do not seek to change the breed Standard, but breed as close to it as is possible, with temperament and soundness the first considerations. Obviously along with this they are getting outstanding quality.

GLINDALE

Glindale Chihuahuas at Harrington Park, New Jersey, are owned by Linda and Joe Glenn, both of whom since early childhood have been great dog fanciers of all breeds. With the creation of the Glindale Kennel name in 1969, the Glenns started out breeding, showing, or just owning Yorkshire Terriers, Old English Sheepdogs, Boston Terriers and Soft Coated Wheaten Terriers. However, their love and devotion to the Chihuahua breed was essentially due to their daughter, Kristen, who in 1977 wrote Santa Claus a special letter requesting a puppy dog which would "never grow up." So it was that on Christmas Day 1977, Santa delivered the Glenns' first Chihuahua, Sampsen. She has fulfilled Kristy's wish, and now, at age eight years, is one of the more famous dogs in the world, who weighs but a mere 20 ounces!

The Glenns' involvement in Chihuahuas has continued and flourished since that snowy Christmas morning. Sampsen, in particular, has provided immeasurable positive value and publicized promotion for the breed. Her lovable disposition and irresistible personality have done their bit to dispel any ill-founded notions about Chihuahua type and disposition which have been lurking in the minds of the public. Linda and Sam have appeared in the *New York Daily News,* the *New York Times,* the *New York Post,* and on several TV shows, among them *Sixty Minutes.* During the Westminster Kennel Club Dog Show in 1982, as a television feature, a special judging for this purpose was arranged by a panel of young dog lovers who chose Sampsen as "Miss Personality of Westminster 1982" over numerous competitors. In attending shows in the northeast area, Sampsen is always immediately recognized upon arrival at ringside, in her custom Poochie Pouch and doll carriage.

Originally based on the Harmony bloodlines of Dave Harmon and Wesley Kellum, the Glindale breeding and show schedule remains very active. Logging several thousand miles of travel each year, the Glenns have achieved considerable success exhibiting their handsome little dogs. With extensive showing over the past few years Glindale has earned Specialty wins in New York, New Jersey, and Maryland.

Currently the more notable Glindale champions are Champion Glindale's Little Bit of Sampsen, who finished with a Westminster Best of Winners; Champion Harmony's Hugabee of Glindale; and American and Bermudian Champion Glindale's Mighty Munchkin. Both Hugabee and Tiny Tan (Munchkin) are multiple Specialty and Best of Variety winners. Tiny obtained his Bermuda title in November 1981 going Best of Variety at four successive shows and placing in the Groups at all four of them over Best in Show and international winners—this at only seven months old and under well-known international judges. The Bermuda Kennel Club, in recognition of Tiny's spectacular feat, also awarded him the special trophies as Best Puppy in Show for all four of these events. Mrs. Glenn comments, "No such award was presented to any puppy of any breed for a previous period of fifteen years."

Tiny remains undefeated as a special in the United States. He earned his U.S.A. championship with straight Specialty majors, finishing with Best of Winners at the prestigious Westminster in 1982 at age 11 months.

Upcoming puppy prospects undoubtedly will provide the Glindale line with some interesting winners for the future.

Both Linda and Joe are active members in numerous regional and national clubs, including the Chihuahua Club of Greater New York, the Chihuahua Club of America, Kennel Club of Northern New Jersey, and the Dog Fanciers Club of New York. Linda is also Secretary of the First Dog Training Club of New Jersey, and is the present Trophy Chairman for the Chihuahua Club of Greater New York.

With the able assistance of their young daughter, Kristy, Linda and Joe give their love to Chihuahuas while carefully planning to build a strong kennel of top winners for the coming years.

GOLDENBAY

Goldenbay Chihuahuas, owned by Pat and Bob Porreca at Pleasanton, California, are described by Pat as being "new on the block" having been actively engaged in breeding Chihuahuas only since about 1980.

Ch. Glindale Mighty Munchkin in an informal shot. Linda M. Glenn, owner, Glindale Chihuahuas.

This is a double "father-daughter" picture of both the people and the Chihuahuas! Handler Mike Diaz (*left*) has the exciting little fawn dog, Best in Show winning Ch. Elh's Mighty Lunar of Dartan taking Best of Breed. Mike's daughter (*right*), Denille Diaz, has the lead on Lunar's daughter, Ch. Golden Bay's Look At Me Hack's, who is taking Best of Winners and Best of Opposite Sex. Both Chihuahuas owned by Pat Porreca, Pleasanton, California.

After graduating from college (Cornell University), Pat decided to take up showing dogs as a hobby. She started out with an Afghan Hound, but before long the decision had been reached that Afghan coats and a single person's social life and career are hardly compatible. So what could be more completely the opposite? A Chihuahua!

Goldenbay is founded on a combination of Duggar, Handwerk, and Dartan lines. The Dartans especially impressed the Porrecas as being the type with which they wished to establish their strain, thus leading them as Pat says, to "mortgage the house" in order to purchase the smashing little dog Champion Ell Mighty Lunar of Dartan, a move which I am certain they have never for a moment regretted, as Lunar, in a little more than two years of showing, chalked up the imposing record of ten Best in Show victories (seven all-breed, three Specialty Shows), 43 times Best in the Toy Group, and multiple additional Group placements. He became the #1 Chihuahua and Top Ten Toy #8 and #9, was a Westminster Best of Variety winner twice, and Show Dog of the Year semi-finalist for the prestigious *Kennel Review* Tournament of Champions 1985. Also in 1985 he was selected to pose and represent Mighty Dog in their 1985 calendar as "Mr. July." "Buddy," as he is known, has truly opened up doors for the Chihuahua breed by his accomplishments, while at the same time remaining a very special pet, which does not always happen with dogs who are so vigorously campaigned.

Buddy is already proving himself to be a sire of true quality, with champions finished from his early litters.

Other of the Chihuahuas who are playing their part in the Goldenbay success story include Hack's Pack Velvet Imp, who is by Champion Duggan's Black Imp ex a daughter of Champion Dingman's Sundance Kid.

There is also Champion Duggan's Black Imp himself, and a notable daughter of Mighty Lunar, Champion Goldenbay's Moonglow of Hack's Pack who has been bringing home splendid honors from the show ring.

For folks who are "new on the block," or even for those who have been here many years, the Porrecas are certainly setting some exciting records in the breed, and seem well on the road to continuing to do so.

H AND J

H and J Chihuahua Kennels were founded in 1979, since which time numerous champions have been finished for Jack and Hilda Phariss under the H and J banner.

Foundation bitch was Gotcher Pretty Ruffles who produced four champions and one major pointed offspring. Two of her sons, in turn, have become champion sires, and her daughter, Champion H and J's Blue Impy, has produced three champions plus one major pointed offspring to date. These numbers will most certainly continue to grow.

Impy's outstanding "kids" include Champion H and J's Mystic

Wizard, a young dog just beginning his specials career. While still in the classes, Rags, as he is known, was Winners Dog at both the Chihuahua Club of America and Houston Chihuahua Club Specialties, and was also named Best Long Coat Puppy in Sweepstakes at the Chihuahua Club of America.

Champion H and J's Perfecta Pan and Champion H and J's Peanut Pan are two outstanding daughters of Champion H and J's Blue Impy. Peanut was awarded Best Smooth Puppy in Sweepstakes at the Chihuahua Club of America Rotating Specialty in Baltimore, Maryland, and is Group-placed in very limited showing as a special.

Champion H and J's Missing Pittore and Champion H and J's Crystal Princess are two excellent litter sisters bred by H and J Kennels. Crystal was Best of Opposite Sex to Best of Variety at the Chihuahua Club of America Fall Specialty and Best of Opposite Sex to Best of Breed at the Dallas Chihuahua Club.

H and J has concentrated on an intensive linebreeding program centered around Champion Pittore's Pompeii Pan, sire of Champion Pittore's Macho Man (#1 Chihuahua in the United States for 1980), Champion Pittore's Lasting Little Hope (multiple Group winner), Champion Pittore's Peter Pan, and Champion Shinybrook Pompeii Pantero. Other individual dogs have been introduced into the program in order to complement type and movement.

Jack Phariss is a practicing attorney and Hilda Phariss is a biology-chemistry teacher by training who has become a municipal court administrator.

HOLIDAY

The Holiday line of Chihuahuas, owned by Mary Myers at Phoenix, Arizona, combine the bloodlines of Varga's, Hurd's, Shroyer, Westwind, Son-Ko, Thurmer, and Bill's. All mixed up and baked into a pretty package! Mrs. Myers feels strongly that a lovely head is important in a Chihuahua, with the classic large dome and large ears and big luminous eyes—characteristics which, in this writer's opinion, many people seem to ignore nowadays.

Mrs. Myers believes that Champion Holiday Punchinella is the one and only *white* Smooth Coat Chihuahua. No one else connected with the National Club knows of any so far as she can ascertain. Having been working since 1979 on development of a

Ch. Holiday's Hershey Bar, by Ch. Varga's Chantelly Casanova ex Varga's Tijuana Chi Chi, is handled here by Jim Lehman for breeder-owner Mary Myers. A popular stud with "children" as far away as Japan, Hershey Bar was Winners Dog at the Michigan Specialty in 1978 and Best of Variety at the Wisconsin Chihuahua Specialty that same year.

white line with dark eye and pigment, she is gratified that her efforts are beginning to take shape. As we write, she has four adult white bitches, two white bitch pups, and a white male. Two of the bitches have black eyes but pink nose. Several times this fancier has traveled considerable distances to see what she has been told are pure white Chihuahuas, only to find them actually to be cream, or white spotted with black or gold. She has had several other pure whites which have been lost for one reason or another, but she will be ceaseless in her efforts to establish a reliable strain of them.

Smooth Coat Chihuahuas are the specialty at Holiday, although a few Long Coats are in residence there, too. The Myers came to Phoenix from their former home in Logansport, Indiana, during the spring of May 1981 to attend the dog shows, fell in love with the place and moved their kennel there in January of 1982.

Most famous of Mrs. Myers' Chihuahuas is Champion Holiday's Tijuana La Cune, who is an all-breed Best in Show winner, a National Specialty Best of Breed winner, has placed in 46 Toy Groups, and has been shown only 86 times. She is the top winning dog owned by the Myers, and the only one they have seriously campaigned. Now she is proving her value in the whelping box, too, already having a couple of champion offspring attracting admiring attention at the shows. These are Holiday Tijuana Johnny, now owned by Mr. Morris Lichtenstein of Corpus Christi, Texas, who became a champion with ease, and Holiday I Love Lucy who was also quick to gain title and is still owned by Mrs. Myers.

Champion Varga's Richardo De Oro, descended from the fabulous Champion Tejano Texas Kid and from Champion Shaw's Little Spunk and Thurmer's Jemima is closely linebred to Champion Rowe's Charama De Oro. Richardo is accorded great credit for the outstanding heads on the Holiday Chihuahuas.

Champion Holiday's Spot Silver and his son Champion Holiday's Ink Spot De Oro are two other stud dogs of merit who have helped create the quality for which Holiday Chihuahuas are famous. Ink Spot is a three-and-a-half pound black, tan and white of tremendous style, while Spot Silver is a stunning blue and white.

Champion Holiday's Hershey Bar is another very worthy little dog bearing this kennel identification. He is only three pounds, chocolate and gold in color, and is the sire of Champion Holiday's

Chantelly Valor and Holiday's Flash Gordon.

HURD'S

The Hurd bloodlines, which have become of such prominence in the Chihuahua world, were founded in 1957 when Max and Marie Hurd of Council Bluffs, Iowa, purchased Thurmer's Tammy Jo, Smooth Coat bitch sired by Champion Thurmer's Hugo II from Tressa E. Thurmer.

Tammy was bred to Champion Thurmer's Danny to produce Thurmer's Keely. Both Tammy and Keely were then bred to Champion Fitch's Tawny Kid (Champion Tejano Texas Kid ex Thurmer's Botchimee) to produce Champion Hurd's Tequilla Kid and Champion Hurd's Starlite, the first two homebred champions produced by the Hurds.

In the meantime, a show prospect puppy male was purchased from Marjorie H. Grosart. This male, Champion Grosart's Rickee Rue, became Hurds' first champion.

These dogs were the foundation of the Hurd Smooth Coat line. Hurds' Long Coats started out on a blend of Stober, Shroyer, and Gehlsen lines.

Many other fine dogs from various kennels were purchased by the Hurds and bred into their original lines over the years. However, the majority of these also went back to the Thurmer, Grosart, and Tejano strains.

Max Hurd has continued breeding and exhibiting Chihuahuas since Marie's death in 1982. Approximately 95 champions have been owned by the Hurds, 65 of whom were homebred. Max's latest special, Champion Dartan's Barbary Coast, was purchased from the breeders, Darwin and Tanya Delaney. "Bart," who was Winners Dog and Best of Winners at the Chihuahua Club of America Specialty and finished his title undefeated, is combining well with the matrons of the Hurd lines, promising to push that count of champions over 100 very shortly.

An especially outstanding little dog has been Champion Hurd's Kojak, who placed his stamp well on many of the winners of the 1970s. He was a great-grandson of Champion Hurd's Lil Indian, so carries the Hurd lines for at least several generations.

Champion Hurd's Honey Bee, from the late 1960s into the 1970s, was #1 Chihuahua in the United States for 1969 and 1970, the winner of two all-breed Bests in Show, first in a dozen Toy

Ch. Hurd's Lil Indian, by Ch. Hurd's Tequilla Kid ex Lana's Mona, Winners Bitch at the Chihuahua Club of America Specialty Show and Toy Group winner was typical of Tequilla Kid's progeny produced during the 1960s. Here handled by the late Clara Alford under judge J.J. Duncan. Breeder, Monte F. Littler. Owner, Max E. Hurd.

Groups, and many other honors, co-owned by breeder Max E. Hurd and Teddye Dearborn.

JP

Although she speaks of herself as still being "very novice to the breed," Judy Padgug, Sacramento, California, is one of our most enthusiastic Long Coat breeders who is also very fond of the Smooth Coats. Previous to getting started with the Chihuahuas, Judy had owned a St. Bernard kennel that was just becoming well established when her marriage broke up, forcing her to sell her kennel and many lovely Saints. She still had the urge to show dogs, though, despite living in an apartment.

In 1980 Judy was at a benched show at the Cow Palace handling a Champion Flat Coated Retriever for a friend, and just happened to pass a crate in which was sitting a beautiful tiny Long Coat Chihuahua bitch. Of course it was love at first sight for Judy, and right then she determined that one of these she *would* have, as it could be easily managed even in the apartment. Unfortunately the little bitch who had caught Judy's attention had just been sold by her breeder, Jan Schroeder. However, there was another litter soon due and Judy was invited to call if still interested when the puppies would have arrived.

Jan and her husband Dan Schroeder are the breeders and owners of Champion Schroeder's Daisy, who is still shown occasionally and successfully in Veteran Classes had not only had a very exciting show career, but has also produced several fine champions.

One day Jan Schroeder called to tell Judy that she had some pups if Judy would care to come look at them. Of course she would, and drove over to the Schroeder home in the Bay area where she fell head over heels in love with one of the puppies. That pup, Mama Lisa as Judy calls her now, soon became Champion JP's Pequena Amiga, and she has not only proven herself an excellent show girl, but has done a fine job of whelping and raising some beautiful pups of her own.

Mama Lisa's first litter was sired by Champion Stober's Erik of Wildwood. This litter produced Macho, Taco, and Dolly. Taco is the cutest and the smallest and a loving pet in addition to turning out to be the most outstanding of the litter. His new owner has no desire to show him. "You guessed it," says Judy, "I sold the pick

Ch. Hurd's Honey Bee was #1 Chihuahua in the U.S.A. for 1969 and 1970. Among outstanding honors were two all-breed Bests in Show (Cedar Rapids K.C. and Littleton Mile Hi) and 12 Toy Group 1sts. Here winning under judge Joe Faigel, handled by Peggy Hogg for owners Max E. Hurd and Teddye Dearborn, bred by Mr. Hurd. Sired by Ch. King's Bounty ex Ch. Hurd's Bit O'Honey.

"Mama Lisa" (Ch. JP's Pequena Amiga) with Dolly, Taco and Macho. Judy Padgug, JP Chihuahuas.

of the litter to a pet home." Of course Macho is pointed and Dolly, the puppy Judy kept, needs only a major now for her championship.

Dolly and Mama Lisa have just recently started showing in brace competition. They are very similar and well matched and won the Long Coat brace at this past year's Chihuahua Club of Northern California Specialty, whence Mama Lisa also came home with several very splendid trophies.

A few months after the birth of that litter, a friend of Judy's decided she wanted a Long Coat, too. So Jan was contacted again, and Huggybear was acquired, who is currently being obedience trained and it is hoped will be ready to start competing this fall. Daily the kids in the neighborhood are knocking at the front door asking to take him for walks. He is quite a solid hit!

Huggybear is linebred out of Daisy and Hurd's Chihuahua linebreeding. Mama Lisa's dam is a half sister to Daisy. So this past April, Huggybear was bred to Mama Lisa. Thus Judy now has Ramba and Rita. Both pups are real sound, and Rancho is a true knockout. Judy hopes to be able to keep him and show him also.

She is planning soon now to purchase some property where she can build a home and small kennel, which she would like to have completed in a few years when she retires from her county job. Then she wants to devote full time to the dogs and showing. We wish her great success in this plan.

JO-EL

Jo-El Chihuahuas at Creve Coeur, Missouri, are owned by Joan and Russ Kruetzman who have raised some very distinguished little dogs there.

Pride of place must, of course, go to the marvelous homebred Champion Jo-El's Drummer Boy, who is a son of Champion Dartan's Pirate Blackbeard ex Thurmer's Little Jayme.

Drummer Boy started his career by becoming the youngest Chihuahua ever to gain titular honors, which he did at age six months and eight days from the Puppy Class on January 13, 1985.

Out as a Special for only four months, Drummer Boy has gained, among other honors, four consecutive Toy Group 1sts plus the thrilling award of an all-breed Best in Show at the Sedalia Kennel Club on July 7, 1985, followed a couple weeks later with Best in Specialty Show at the Chihuahua Club of Greater Milwaukee.

Considering his extreme youth and the success with which he has already met, it would seem a safe prediction that Drummer Boy will go down in history as one of the breed's most successful and exciting winners.

Champion Jo-El's Livin' Doll is also sired by Pirate Blackbeard. She, like Drummer Boy, is a homebred, and was hand-raised as her mother died at Doll's birth necessitating that she be tube-fed hourly. The Kruetzmans are being well rewarded for their effort, as Doll completed her championship at ten months and has three Group placements to date.

The sire of these two "stars," Champion Dartan's Pirate Blackbeard, was acquired by the Kruetzmans from his breeders, Tanya and Darwin Delaney. Pirate himself has earned some mighty impressive honors, such as Best in the Chihuahua Club of America's record 275 entry Specialty Show during October 1984; becoming the #3 ranked Smooth Coat for 1984; and having also been a Top Producer for 1984. Definitely the sort of dog one wants in their kennel!

KOMO

Komo Chihuahuas are owned by Katherine J. Hood of Altamont, Illinois, who is a registered nurse and a retired art instructor of considerable talent as anyone who has ever seen her paintings and drawings will be quick to state.

It was in 1972, following her divorce, that Mrs. Hood became interested in breeding and showing Chihuahuas, selecting as her foundation stock representatives of the Shroyer and Thurmer bloodlines. Since that time she has proven her knowledge as a breeder, with at least 40 champions having been finished, mostly bred, owned, and handled personally. Her principal stud dog to date has been the very dominant sire, Champion Komo's Tao Amo, by Jackson's Ohio Mobea ex Thurmer's Suzette. This little dog, now 12 years of age, is the sire, grandsire, or great grandsire of all the Komo champions, as the entire kennel is linebred to him. In addition to those already sporting titles, there are numerous others on the way, a number of whom should have joined the finished champions by the time you are reading this.

Probably Komo's most exciting year to date has been 1983, during which Mrs. Hood finished nine champions, which is certainly an achievement in which any breeder can well take pride.

Returning to the kennel's early days, in addition to owning Champion Komo's Tao Amo, Mrs. Hood also acquired a litter sister to this dog, Champion Komo's Mya Keta. These two really brought the cream of Chihuahua bloodlines with them, tracing back to Champion Shroyers Rebel Robin on the sire's side, and to Champions Thurmer's Hugo, Jose Hombre and Sheba, all the way back to Champion Tejano Texas Kid on the dam's side.

Current winners at Komo, or from there, include Champion Komo's Tao Yan Kee Wee MCG, owned by T. Silva, who has been doing well in the Alabama area, and Champion Komo's Tao Harlequin Burl, Esq., owned by La Duc Chihuahuas.

Mrs. Lloyd Reeves, who was among this country's Chihuahua breeder-exhibitors of the 1930s and who has shared her interests with several breeds over the years (including Dalmatians where her Tattoo Kennels are world famous), has been winning well recently with several Chihuahuas purchased from and shown by Katherine Hood. Notable among these are Champion Komo's Tao Skylark Serenade, Champion Komo's Tao Mya Cheta Tattoo,

Ch. Jo-El's Drummer Boy, a homebred Best in Show winner from Jo-El Kennels, Joan and Russ Kruetzman. Best in Show, all breeds, Sedalia K.C. 1985, handler Terri Lydden. Best in Specialty Show Chihuahua Club of Milwaukee 1985. Consistent winner of Group 1sts.

51

Ch. Komo's Tao Wagtime Cowboy taking Best of Opposite Sex in Long Coats at the Atlanta Specialty in 1984. Bred and owned by Katherine J. Hood, Altament, Illinois.

Champion Komo's Tao C.C. Castinetta, and Champion Komo's Tao D'Lovely Ora Lee who finished at six years of age and has produced a quite sensational youngster in Komo's Tao Apple Jackie. Mrs. Reeves has also another splendid youngster, Komo's Tao Truly Flair. Looks as though both Mrs. Hood and Mrs. Reeves will be enjoying these "young hopefuls" in the near future.

MICLANJO

Miclanjo Chihuahuas at Rockville, Maryland, were established in the spring of 1968 with the purchase, by the John Mooneys, of two Smooth puppies from Muriel Jones. They were Mooney's Mighty Imp and Mooney's Little Bit, the latter eventually becoming a C.D.X. titleholder, among her successes a First placement in Open B Competition.

It was Little Bit who produced the first of the homebred champions for the Mooneys in her first litter, whom they named Mooney's Dinah Mite.

The kennel name Miclanjo was created from the names of the Mooney children, MIchael, CLayton, ANgela and JOhn, most of whom were or still are actively involved with showing the dogs.

After several comparatively quiet years with their Chihuahuas, while the family was busy with such matters as retiring from the Air Force, completion of college degrees and establishing new careers, Miclanjo returned to the show ring stronger and in better style than ever during the latter part of 1983. 1984 saw five new champions finished under the Miclanjo banner, including the multiple Group-placing Champion Miclanjo Wilhewag of Lazy VK. Willie's first daughter has finished in 1985, and other of his kids are winning well as we write.

One of the very famous earlier winners at this kennel was Champion Mooney's SuCie Miclanjo who earned Best of Variety at the Chihuahua Club of Oklahoma Specialty under breeder-judge Alberta Booth and Toy Group 3rd at Faith City Kennel Club under Gus Wolf. These wins, along with numerous Best of Variety wins at other shows, earned her the rating of Top Winning Long Coat Chihuahua Bitch in 1973.

In April 1984, SuCie came out of retirement to attend some Specialty Shows in the Veterans Class. Her score was several exciting Veterans wins, plus being among the very first winners of a Hill's Science Diet Senior Award.

Champion Miclanjo Kaleidescope was born in August 1984. She finished at age ten months and with three majors gained under such noted judges as Ruth Terry (5 points) and Dr. Leon Seligman (4 points). She is a daughter of Champion Miclanjo's Wilhewag of Lazy VK ex Lazy VK's Trinket Miclanjo.

Champion Miclanjo Wilhewag of Lazy VK started his show career at the Chihuahua Club of Maryland Specialty with a reserve to a 5-point major at barely six months' age. His first Group wins were back-to-back placements during the latter part of 1984, and his successes that year earned him a #4 and #5 in the ranking systems for that year.

Champion Lazy VK Caroline Miclanjo finished her title at 14 months, with a Group placement following quickly her first time out as as special, which was also Michael Mooney's first time out there.

"Carrie" has free-whelped two promising litters, one of four puppies, the second of five puppies, proving herself a good little mother as well as a lovely showgirl.

In 1985 she has been shown on only eight occasions, taking Best of Variety at seven of these shows.

MIGNON'S

Mignon's Chihuahuas are owned by Mignon Murray of Jacksonville, Florida, who formerly was located in the New York area. For many years Mignon was a leading professional handler, and there are more than 100 Chihuahuas on whom she put the title of "champion" for her clients.

As is usually the case when one handles dogs for others, Mignon's own Chihuahuas were forced to take a back seat while all this was going on. However, since completing title on Champion Karlena's TVP Pulgada during 1951, she has shown more than 20 of her own Chihuahuas not only to their titles but to some excellent wins as well.

In 1970 Mignon turned her interest to judging, applying for A.K.C. approval to do so, which was promptly granted. This is a very knowledgeable "dog lady" who has much talent to offer in our rings; that this fact is known and appreciated is pointed up by her ever growing popularity.

Mignon is becoming increasingly interested in horses, which share her time now with the dogs.

OKATOMA

Okatoma Chihuahuas are owned by Patricia Lambert and her family who live alongside the river just north of Hattiesburg, Mississippi, the river for which the kennel was named. The family consists of Rae Ann and Stan Lambert, Jr., Nancy Lambert, age 12, and Patricia who is 22 and the one primarily involved with the Chihuahuas. The entire family shares a love of the Chihuahuas, along with the responsibility of the busy boarding kennel which they operate. Patricia is especially in charge of the Chihuahua activities, plus managing the boarding kennel. She is a dog obedience instructor (Fonzie, C.D.X., was trained and handled by her) and also loves the competition in conformation classes, where both Champion "Classy" and Champion "Bita" were finished to their titles by her.

Rae Lambert assists in all phases, keeps the books, and it is she who trained "Whiskey," C.D., and made a bench champion of "Skeeter."

Ch. Mignon's Danny Duvall winning Best of Variety at Westminster K.C. in 1976. Mignon Murray, owner-handler.

Ch. Okatoma Herron's I've Got Class, handled by her breeder- owner, Patricia Lambert, taking Best of Winners at Mobile, Alabama, in 1984 under popular Chihuahua breeder judge Arlene Thompson.

Stan adds moral support, checks boarders in and out when available, and generally helps keeps things running smoothly.

The Lamberts are fairly new to the Chihuahua world, but have very definitely come a long way in a short time. Their first registered Chihuahua was purchased in 1980. Yet already they have finished three champions all of whom are homebred, have two already titled obedience degree holders with more on the way, and are especially proud of their two Group winners and their Top 10 Obedience Chihuahuas.

Although the Lamberts own and operate their small all-breed boarding kennel, the Chihuahuas all are basically house dogs, the Chihuahua family consisting of ten.

Okatoma Chihuahuas were founded on a mixture of several excellent lines. Their best brood bitch, "Whiskey" (Pete's Whiskey Lady, C.D.) is a granddaughter of Varga's Tiojana Brass, and she is the dam of Champion Okatoma's Lickidy Split (Skeeter), and of Champion Okatoma's Little Bita Whiskey (Bita).

The other foundation bitches go back to Herron, Hurds, Kitty's and Luce plus a few others. As Patricia comments, "We did not really start with a specific line," but they are well pleased with the way things are working out.

Among the conformation champions at the kennel in addition to "Skeeter" and "Bita" is "Classy," or, more formally, Champion Okatoma Herron's I've Got Class. She was breeder-owner-handled to her title, and is by Herron's CR Sandman ex Lacey's Carmalita. Sandman, incidentally, is also the sire of Champion Okatoma's Little Bita Whiskey.

"Bita" finished her title in nine shows going Best of Breed for her first four majors. She has a Group 2nd under Norman Patton and a Group 4th under Mr. Fields, all prior to her nine-month birthday!

Champion Okatoma's Lickidy Split, or "Champion Skeeter" to her family, finished from the puppy classes and should be in the obedience ring about the time I am writing, where it is hoped (and expected) that she will carry on in the family tradition.

The youngest of the show dog department as we write is "Gizmo," or Okatoma's Blaze Away Gremlin, who at eight months has already a Group placement under Mrs. V. M. Olivier. "Gizmo" is by Champion Ellen's Little Blaze Bandito ex Wee

Windsom Windy, and was bred by Pat Rose and Jean Norton.

And then we have "Fonzie," who is in public life Okatoma's Mr. Cool, C.D.X. This splendid little son of Jackie's Little Sugar Daddy ex Lacey's Wee Botiqua, was bred and trained by Pat Lambert, his owner, and he was one of the Top Ten Obedience Chihuahuas for 1984. He is now in training for Utility.

OZ

The Oz Kennel of Chihuahuas was founded in 1969 by H. William Ohman and Richard G. Racheter who bred these fine dogs until 1977 when Annette Mellinger of Matawan, New Jersey, became their partner upon their retirement from active participation in the Fancy. Since then Mrs. Mellinger and her son, Eric, who now, in 1985 at 20 years of age, is a third year Cadet at the USAF Academy in Colorado Springs, Colorado, where he is becoming an astronautical engineer, continue to breed and show the Oz Chihuahuas.

The Mellingers tell us that to date over 70 Oz champions have been produced, despite the fact that breeding is always on a limited basis, remaining strictly within the Oz strain, and all home bred. It is very rare for them ever to go outside their original line, and only when an outcross has been Oz-sired, then used to breed back to Oz. As Mrs. Mellinger says, "We do not buy our champions from others. Our champions are bred and shown by Oz."

Champion Forest View's Lucky of Oz, "Woody" to his friends, was the Oz foundation dog. First shown at five years' age at the Westbury Kennel Association in 1967, he won a three-point major, finishing his championship eight months later. The first of "Woody's" litters from Betty Lou of Nixon Acres was born on June 22, 1968; all became champions. These were Champion Lucky's Mr. Terri Bubble of Oz (who was Best of Variety at Westminster in 1970); Champion Lucky's Mr. Woody of Oz; and Champion Lucky's Miss Betty Lou of Oz.

His second litter was out of Forest View Snowy Kee Dusto, a daughter of Betty Lou of Nixon Acres, and consisted of four puppies. Again there were three completing titles: Champion Lucky's Electra of Oz who became an international champion; Champion Lucky's Junior Woodsman of Oz who was Best of Variety at Westminster in 1971, and Champion Lucky's Miss Glinda of Oz, Best of Opposite Sex at Westminster in 1971 and #3 Long Coat Chihuahua in 1971 Phillips System. Mrs. Mellinger notes that this was the only occasion to her knowledge when Long Coat Chihuahua littermates have been Best of Variety and Best of Opposite Sex at the same Westminster Kennel Club Show.

When Woody was bred to his half sister, Forest View's St. Susan of Oz, who was another daughter of Betty Lou of Nixon Acres, the entire litter of four males all obtained their titles. These were Champion Lucky's St. George of Oz, Champion Lucky's St. Star of Oz, Champion Lucky's Mr. St. Ojo of Oz, and Champion Lucky's Mr. St. Bojo of Oz. By the time of Woody's death, he had already sired 25 champions.

Woody was awarded the Dog World Award of Canine Distinction on May 10, 1977.

As for Betty Lou of Nixon Acres, she became dam of ten Long Coat Champions, and in 1970 was named a Top Producer of Distinction among all-breeds. Two of her daughters, Forest View Snowy-Kee-Dusto and Forest View's St. Susan of Oz also became Top Producers. "Suzie" produced seven male champions. "Dusty" produced five champions.

In 1970, Irene C. Khatoonian named The House of Oz a Kennel of Distinction for its record in Long Coat Chihuahuas.

Other distinguished Long Coat champions from the House of Oz include Champion Lucky's Clystmnestra of Oz, who was the dam of four champions, among them, finished in 1973, Champion Pittore's Miz Mini Mouse, who is now owned by Annette Mellinger and Pat Kirms.

Champion Mignon's Beauford is another important Long Coat who was bred by Oz. He is now owned by Dickie Dickerson, whose kennel includes numerous Oz dogs.

Oz Kennels are well-known for Long Coat Chihuahuas of soundness, long silky coats, and attractive snow white coloring splashed with chocolate as well as blue and tan.

The Mellingers are truly dog lovers, placing the welfare of their dogs above the importance of show success. Their home is filled with senior citizens ranging in age from 11 to 14 years of age, who remain beloved family pets. Most of these have all their teeth and are happy and healthy. Breeding at the House of Oz is done only to provide the owners with pups for themselves to show. Pet males are sold and an occasional show puppy goes to a carefully researched show home. The stud dogs are used only by people

This delightful head-study is of Ch. Pittore's Miz Minnie Mouse, bred by Oz Kennels and owned by A. Mellinger and Pat Kirns.

whom the Mellingers have learned to know and trust—those who love the dog first and the glory of winning second. Dogs are never bred or advertised by the kennel for sale.

Annette Mellinger and her husband Dan are both school teachers, as Annette says, "to earn our daily bread and our little kids' dog biscuits." Mrs. Mellinger is Secretary of the Chihuahua Club of Mid-Jersey and a member of the Chihuahua Club of America. Also they belong to the Union County Kennel Club and to the Chihuahua Club of Greater New York. They are active in the breeding of Chinese Crested dogs as well as Chihuahuas, and Annette is Secretary of the Chinese Crested Club of Central New Jersey as well.

Since 1977 when Mrs. Mellinger took over at Oz, homebred champions have included the following: Champion Lucky's Dicky Chip of Oz, Champion Eric's Joe Louis Chip of Oz, Champion Eric's Benji Chip of Oz, Champion Eric's C. P. Chip of Oz, Champion Myways Nip Tuck of Oz, Champion Lucky's Antigoni of Oz, Champion Eric's Lucky Casper Rex of Oz, Champion Eric's Previous Munchkin Chip of Oz, Champion Eric's Peter Munchkin, Champion Don Jacquin Federico Chanel. Lucky Eric's Electra of Oz and Eric's Misty Blue of Oz are among their outstanding youngsters on the way to the title.

PITTORE

Pittore's Chihuahuas are widely known around the world for their excellence of quality, type and soundness, and have done an impressive amount of winning for their owner and in the majority of cases their breeder, Patricia H. Pittore of Goshen, Massachusetts.

Pat Pittore acquired her first member of this breed in 1947 as a gift, and it was about 13 years later when she decided that she would like to raise them. Her success has been phenomenal, as she has established a line of Smooth Coats that has racked up a formidable number of champions and important winners. By now her total number of champions finished must be reaching close to 100 with an additional several dozen who were bred by her, finished by other owners. Her enthusiasm for the breed is deep and sincere, as is that of Joyce McComiskey who handles so many of them for her. Pat's schedule is a full one which does not always permit the time she would like to have to devote to showing dogs.

The foundation of the Pittore Kennels was finished to become its first champion in 1964, champion Ty-Bay's Blue Impy, who is behind probably about 65% of the Pittore champions. Her second champion bitch, Clivia's Farfalla Carla, is behind close to 50% of them.

Among the noted winners, Champion Pittore's Walking Tall ac-:ounted for five Toy Group Firsts and 12 additional group placements. Champion Pittore's Macho Man has done well for himself in Specialty Show and Group competition. Champion Pittore's Saber Dancer (sired by Champion Duggers Disco Dancer and himself the sire of the currently winning Champion Pittore's Harvest Dancer) is another Group winner from this kennel, as is Champion Pittore's Lasting Little Hope.

Champion Pittore's Harvest Dancer has been really going full steam ahead, with wins which include Best of Breed at the 1985 National Specialty, Group firsts and placements, and Best of Variety at the A.K.C. Centennial Dog Show in Philadelphia during November 1984.

PRATT'S

Pratt's Kennels were established many years ago by Dorothy Pratt, who has been showing dogs since the early 1940s, and her husband. Mrs. Pratt's first dog show was at San Antonio in 1942. She and her husband later became professional handlers, but at that period wartime made travel to dog shows almost impossible, thus they were able to make only the shows which were nearby. Mrs. Pratt recalls, with nostalgia, Clara Alford showing the wonderful Champion Tejano's Texas Kid for Mrs. Roberts, and also the Pratts lived, in those days, just down the street from Mrs. Attas for several years. However, they did not become involved with Chihuahuas until 1976, when Mr. Pratt spent a year in a wheel chair, and wanted a small dog who could sit on his lap and a Chihuahua was selected. By now Chihuahuas have become so integral a part of the Pratts' everyday life that they feel almost as though the years they spent showing Poodles, Yorkshire Terriers, Maltese, Greyhounds, and various other breeds were wasted as the Chihuahuas do not have the same type coats which are a constant care, and thus can be truly enjoyed.

Getting into Chihuahuas was easy for the Pratts, as Mrs. Pratt had observed much about them when living in Texas. Also, the noted Poodle handler Jordan Chamberlain grew up grooming Poodles for Mrs. Pratt. So when Jordan went to take over at Round Table Kennels, he acquired for Mrs. Pratt the lovely little eight-week-old dog Round Table Mr. Bojangles. By the time Jordan sent Bojangles to the Pratts, who were then located in Lakeland, Florida, where they now live, the little dog was already a champion. The Pratts sent him out with Glynette Cass and he became #5 Long Coat Chihuahua for 1980. His show successes include 150 times Best of Variety.

The Pratts' other good fortune at this time was knowing Joyce McComiskey for some thirty odd years, as it was from her that they purchased Champion Lakeview Leprechaun as their foundation Smooth. This dog has produced eight champions for the Pratts and his progeny are also producing champions.

Mrs. Hale was practically a neighbor, and it was from her that the Pratts acquired Champion Pratt's Hale Festus Haggan, son of her Top Producing dog, Champion Hale's Bonansa Little Joe.

By now the Pratts are establishing their own line by using Lakeview, Hale, and Pittore lines together. They have, just as we are writing, an eight- month, three-day-old male who is the second generation of their own breeding, Champion Pratt's Tiny Tim.

Mrs. Pratt feels that she can now say the Pratts have a line of their own, but not without the friendship and guidance from such friends as Jordan Chamberlain, Myrle Hale, Joyce McComiskey, and Pat Pittore. For awhile now, Dorothy Pratt has looked forward to raising some top quality show Chis, using the knowledge gained during her 43 years of raising show Poodles and the other breeds with which she has been involved. From the look of things, we would say that she is off to a splendid start in this direction.

QUACHITAH

Quachitah Chihuahuas, owned and handled by Linda George at Waukesha, Wisconsin, have become renowned for some of the most notable accomplishments in the entire world of Chihuahuas.

Take for instance Champion Quachitah For Your Eyes Only, a homebred son of Champion Dartan's Elfin Magic ex Champion Quachitah Sundrop. This splendid little dog, an owner-handled homebred, was Group 1st at the Westminster Kennel Club Dog Show in February 1984, defeating many of the leading names in the Toy World during this decade. It was the first such victory for

Pratt's Chocolate Muchacho, three-pound chocolate and tan Smooth male, winning a major at Valdosta, Florida, 1985. Dorothy A. Pratt, owner.

Ch. Pratt's Dare To Be Great, black and tan Smooth female, finished in 1984 for owner Dorothy A. Pratt.

any Chihuahua at this most prestigious of all American dog shows, and the third time only that a member of the breed has even placed in the Toy Group there.

But that was only one of a long series of spectacular successes for this great dog! Four times he has been selected as Best in Show in keen all-breed competition. In addition, twice during his career he has been Best of Breed at the Chihuahua Club of America National Specialty.

There are three other Chihuahuas at Quachitah as well who have won all-breed Bests in Show for their owner, all personally handled by her. They include Champion Quantico's Daisy Mae, by Canadian Champion Pierre E of Quantico ex Quantico's Satin Sinner, bred by Mrs. C. G. Peterson. In addition to her own exciting show career, Daisy Mae is the dam of International Champion Quachitah Adonis, an All-Breed and Specialty Best in Show winner in Mexico, whom Linda George bred and who she now co-owns. Adonis, in his turn, is the sire of another All-Breed Best in Show-winning Chihuahua in Mexico.

Champion Dartan Dominique D'Quachitah, by Champion Quachitah Apocalypse ex Champion Dartan's Calamity Jane, was bred by Darwin and Tanya Delaney and is now owned and handled by Linda George. Dominique also is an All-Breed and Specialty Best in Show winner.

Still another familiar face in the All-Breed Best in Show circle is Champion Quachitah Fire and Ice by Champion Quachitah Apocalypse ex Champion Quantico's Shalele.

Quachitah Chihuahuas are primarily descended from the Dartan and Quantico lineage. They have all been owner-handled to their many Group and Best in Show wins, and have certainly more than made their presence felt no matter how keen the competition.

In addition to her Best in Show dogs, Linda George also owns the following Toy Group winners:

Champion Quantico's Bluebell, who is the granddam of three All-Breed Best in Show winners; Champion Quachitah Diamonds "R" Forever, who sired Champion For Your Eyes Only; and the lovely Long Coat, Champion Sandi-Lee's Little Bear Bryant.

ROUND TABLE

Round Table Chihuahuas were owned by the late Mrs. Caroline

Keene of Delaware who, with her husband Alden, was a famous Poodle breeder. Chihuahuas very actively shared Mrs. Keene's interest with the Poodles, and one of them, Champion Round Table The One and Only, had a sensational show career handled by Jordan L. Chamberlain.

"Dewey" to friends, Champion Round Table's One and Only had the distinction of winning Best of Breed at the Chihuahua Club of America Specialty Show in Chicago during October 1978 over an entry of 215 Chihuahuas assembled for the opinion of the noted authority Thelma Grey of Rozavel fame on what was probably Mrs. Grey's last assignment in the United States prior to her death, after first winning Best of Variety among Long Coats under Mr. Merrill Cohen.

Champion Round Table's One and Only is one of about 15 Chihuahua champions bred by Mrs. Keene. She dearly loved the breed and always marveled at their stamina.

From Dewey's handler, Jordan L. Chamberlain, comes the information that this gorgeous little dog won a total of three Specialty Shows and a goodly number of Group placements of which at least four were Group 1st. A true "personality dog," Dewey was very widely admired by judges and Chihuahua fanciers alike, adding many new friends to those who appreciate and enjoy these great "big-little" dogs.

SHINYBROOK

Shinybrook Kennels, at Westmoreland, New Hampshire, are owned by Nancy Shonbeck who acquired her first Chihuahuas in 1957, raising them along with her three sons. Although now a grandmother, she still is as keenly as ever interested in her dogs, getting just as much kick out of every anticipated litter and the puppies now as she did in the beginning.

The foundation stock for Shinybrook came from Attas, Traeumer, and Scott breeding, with emphasis originally on the Smooths. To the foundation lines some of Pat Pittore's excellent dogs were soon added, followed more recently by Long Coats from the Pittore Kennels, the La Ora lines, and Oz. Mrs. Shonbeck does breed the two coat varieties together upon occasion. One of the puppies produced from interbreeding is Shinybrook Razamataz, who came from a Long Coat sire and a Smooth dam.

Always Mrs. Shonbeck has a picture in her mind's eye of the

Ch. Quantico's Daisy Mae is an all-breed and Specialty Best in Show winner. Owned by Linda George, Waukesha, Wisconsin.

ideal Chihuahua she wishes to produce. Her philosophy of breeding is "to produce show quality with pet personalities," and her fence climbers become her greatest favorites, as she does "abhor a dumb dog."

Mrs. Shonbeck keeps 20 to 30 Chihuahuas in an attached kennel, a detached kennel, and the kitchen—sometimes a few even in the bedroom. She is the owner of a farm which she runs on a full-time basis (which is why she gets to few dog shows), and herself assumes the responsibility of haying and fencing and cutting the winter's wood.

The greatest pride of Shinybrook Kennels is the lovely Smooth, Champion Shinybrook Peter Panache, whose wins include Winners Dog at Tidewater Kennel Club in November 1984, handled by Joyce McComiskey, and at the A.K.C. Centennial that same month handled by Patricia Pittore. He is a son of Mexican and American Champion Pittore's Peter Pan ex Shinybrook Miz Buz, and is a little dog with whom any breeder would be well pleased.

Champion Shinybrook Charisma Captain is a Long Coat black and white who was winner at the 1985 Chihuahua Club of Michigan Specialty, and Winners Dog at the Chihuahua Club of America Spring Specialty, sired by Lucky's Love Buttons of Oz ex Shinybrook Charisma Mina.

Back in 1979, Shinybrook Pompei Pantero won the New York Specialty for Mrs. Shonbeck.

Champion Shinybrook Ginger Snap started out as a puppy owned by Mrs. Shonbeck, then later was sold to Jeff Nokes in Anaheim, California, for whom she became a champion.

TERRYMONT

Terrymont Chihuahuas are owned by Herbert and E. Ruth Terry at Weston, Connecticut, specialists for many years in the breeding and showing of outstanding conformation and obedience winners. The Terrys' involvement with this breed has been a long one, during which time their dogs have gained fame and admiration in the United States and Canada, having fared outstandingly well both places in both types of competition.

Among the noted Chihuahuas owned by the Terrys over the years have been the Long Coats, Champion Terrymont Peach Parfait (Champion Luce's Tony Tango ex Champion Terrymont Maple Sugar Candy) who was born in May 1964, and littermate

Shinybrook Razamataz, a chocolate and white dog whose obvious quality makes it clear that he could easily have been a champion had not lack of time prevented his owner campaigning him. He belongs to Shinybrook Chihuahuas.

Champion Terrymont Beau Jamie.

Champion Terrymont Trifle of Candy, C.D.X., was a distinguished homebred born in 1963 by Champion Farriston Good and Gay ex Farriston Candy of Terrymont, C.D.

Mrs. Terry is an extremely popular judge nowadays, and as vitally interested as ever in Chihuahuas.

Terrymont Chihuahuas still continue in the winners circle, many of them co-owned or co-bred by the Terrys with Marcia Greenburg. Also Susan Fischer Payne is winning well with little dogs from the Terrymont foundation.

TINY MITE

Tiny Mite Chihuahuas were established in 1952 by Robert L. DeJonge and his wife Helen, of Zeeland, Michigan, and have earned a position of respect in the Chihuahua world for their many generations of homebred champions, both Long Coats and Smooths.

Down through the years, Tiny Mite has bred for medium sized, refined, pretty headed little dogs. Margaret Kraus handled for the DeJonges over a goodly period of time. Since her illness and

Smooth Coat littermates who took Winners Dog and Winners Bitch at the Chihuahua Club of Greater New York Specialty Show in 1983 under Mrs. Geraldine Hess, then went on to complete their titles. Ch. Terrymont Marsubri Chippety (*left*) owned by Mary Ann Minervino; Ch. Terrymont Marsubri Tango (*right*), owners James and Susan Fischer Payne. Breeders, Terrymont Kennels and Marcia Greenburg.

retirement a dozen or so years ago as we write, Jim Lehman has taken over in this department very successfully.

Tiny Mite is a strongly homebred line. Mr. DeJonge tells us that through all these years only two of the Chihuahuas they have shown have been other than homebred. The first of their champions was Champion Tiny Mite's El Pepita, by Tiny Mite's Amber Gem ex Tiny Mite's Estrallita, who gained the title in six shows undefeated in his sex. "Peppy's" half brother, Champion B-Beg's Mitee Koko, also gained title with ease. Both of these became producers of champions.

Now in the 1980s, Champion Tiny Mite's Tag-a-Long gained his title with five-point majors in three separate areas of the United States, having done so by taking Winners Dog at the Chi-

Robert L. DeJonge, breeder-owner, with some of his noted Chihuahuas. These two are Ch. Tiny Mite's Sweetums, by Am., Can., and Ber. Ch. So Big of Remor ex Ch. Tiny Mite's Valentine; and Ch. Tiny Mite's Wee Joy Terrific, by Ch. Tiny Mite's Terrific ex Tiny Mite's La Shasta Ru.

These Chihuahua puppies are by Ch. Will O'Wisp Lil Boy Buttons ex Ch. Will O'Wisp Lil Bonbon Bunny and are owned by Millie F. Williams, Spokane, Washington.

huahua Club of Michigan, the Chihuahua Club of Mid-Jersey, and the Chihuahua Club of Dallas, Texas. Tag-a-Long is by Champion Tiny Mite's Terrific (the sire of seven champions) ex Champion Tiny Mite's Valentine (the dam of six champions).

Most of the Smooth Coats at Tiny Mite are fawn or red-fawn color with jet black eyes and nose. The Long Coats are red, fawn, or chocolate with fawn markings. The DeJonges believe theirs to be one of the finest bloodlines of chocolates in the United States today. The kennel includes numerous champions, some of which are usually to be found in show ring competition.

WILL O'WISP

Will O'Wisp Chihuahuas at Spokane, Washington, are owned by Millie F. Williams who breeds, owns, and handles both long-coated and smooth coated winners.

Champion Will O'Wisp Li'l Boy Buttons is a Long Coat male who started out his career in 1984 at the Chihuahua Club of Maryland under judge Dr. T. Allen Kirk in the 6-9 months class from where he went on to Reserve Winners Dog. The following day at the Chihuahua Club of America Specialty Show in Baltimore, Maryland, he was Best in the Puppy Classes at the Specialty and Best Puppy in Sweepstakes, this time under Dr. William Field, Jr. Winners Dog on the latter occasion was another Long Coat of Will O'Wisp breeding no longer owned by Mrs. Williams.

After that exciting start, Buttons quickly gained his championship within a three-month period under judges Frances Thornton, Frank Nishimura, Dr. William Houpt, Bonnie Brookins, and Langdon Skarda, the latter win as a Chihuahua Specialty supported entry. Buttons has been campaigned as a special on a limited basis, his owner having found that judges seem to prefer the more flashily colored Long Coats to the fawn which is what this little dog is. To Mrs. Williams, and to many others of us, this color has always been especially associated with the Chihuahua breed. Buttons has already sired several litters as we write, which include some puppies for which his owner's hopes are high.

Champion Will O'Wisp Li'l Ruff N Rowdi is a Smooth who has also made his presence felt at the shows. He is a darker fawn than Buttons, who started his career just shortly past age six months in the puppy class, winning four consecutive majors at shows in Montana under judges Michele Billings, Erica Thomsen, Cynthia Sommers, and V. O. Oliver, finishing at his next two shows under Ken McDermott and Paula Bradley. Rowdi is just one year old (September 1985), so will do a bit of maturing before starting out on his specials career.

Myers Cindy Lou II at Camden County K.C. in 1960. Handled by Betty Munden for owner, Carrie S. Myers.

Chapter 4

Some Early Best in Show Chihuahuas

The winning of a Best in Show award is the dream of all who breed and show purebred dogs. Chihuahua folks are no exception; and although it was not until the 1950s, according to our records, that the breakthrough to this honor first came to the breed, Chihuahua fanciers now have a very respectable number of such victories in which to take pride. Remember that the going for so tiny a dog is not always easy, as some judges seem to look for the most showy and glamorous contender in the ring. Actually it was slow going before *any* of the Toy breeds began bringing home the Best in Show victories, but now that they are under way, many of our biggest and most prestigious dog shows are being won by representatives of the Toy Group.

In the kennel stories, you have found specific references to the Best in Show Chihuahuas who have been winning within the past dozen or so years; and they are satisfactorily numerous. What concerns us here are the *earlier* winners—the trailblazers who were the start of Chihuahua recognition in all-breed competition.

The very first to make the breakthrough was Champion Attas's Gretchen who gained her first Best in Show awards for herself and her breed in 1951 and who retired eventually with three such vic-

A reproduction of the advertisement of Mrs. Harry S. Peaster's famous kennel, La Rex Doll Kennels in Philadelphia, Pennsylvania.

tories, plus three Specialty Bests in Show, and twice she was Best American-bred in Show, an award which has since been eliminated. Gretchen was owned and handled by Mrs. Mike Attas of Temple, Texas, from that lady's leading brood matron, Attas' Chipola. It is interesting to note that the bloodlines on which Mrs. Attas's foundation stock were built included some of the La Rex Doll strain owned by Mrs. Harry S. Peaster of Philadelphia, Pennsylvania, whose excellence we have already referred to earlier in this volume. For close to half a century Mrs. Attas had winning dogs in the ring.

In 1952 Champion La May's Dagmar, Champion Shadwick's Romona, Champion La Oro Cajaro De Oro, Champion Miss Rose Bud, and Champion Galvern's Mona added their names to the Best in Show roster. Then, in 1954, along came Champion Tejano's Texas Kid who opened new doors to his breed when he trotted off with All Breed Best in Show honors on *15 occasions* between September 1954 and June 9, 1956. Texas Kid attracted the attention and admiration of judges who I am sure never in the world thought that one day a Chihuahua would win Best in Show under them. He fairly brought down the house when he appeared in the ring, for his style, balance, soundness, ideal action and dauntless personality. Here was a dog to be *noticed*. And that is what he became! He and Clara Alford comprised the team. They will never be forgotten by those who love this breed.

Other memorable Best in Show Chihuahuas of the 1950s included Champion McCasland Melodia, C.D., American and Canadian Champion Hogan's Amigo, and Champion Buck's Jetta.

The 1960s saw some new stars arise on the horizon. Champion Kottke's Little Sweety Pie for one; Champion Kitty's Miss Brag About; Champion Gindon Bo Jangles; Champion Gene's Carla and Champion Thurmer's Little Gayla.

Still further frosting was added to the cake during the 1970s with the seven Bests in Show won by the diminutive and dainty Long Coat, Champion Snow Bunny d'Casa de Cris, whose record also included 88 Group placements of which 33 were first, or Best in Group. Snow Bunny was #1 Chihuahua in the United States for 1975 and 1976, #6 Toy Dog and #37 all breeds for 1976, *Kennel Review* System. In the *National Dog* rating system she was #1 Chihuahua and #6 Toy Dog for both 1975 and 1976; and she was #1 Long Coat Chihuahua, both systems, for 1977. She was bred, owned, and handled by Martha Hooks, Birmingham, Alabama.

Champion Quantico's Little Crusader won four all-breed Bests in Show between October 1972 and March 1974. Along with these wins he earned 80 Group placements and was #1 Smooth Chihuahua for 1972, 1973, and 1974. This was believed to be the top record for an *owner-handled* Smooth Coat at that time in breed history. Crusader defeated 20,000 dogs in four years. Additionally he is the sire of some outstanding champions.

Champion Hurd's Honey Bee won a Best in Show in June 1970. Champion Margate's Little Bit of Speed did so as well, and the same is true of Champion Quantico's Daisy Mae.

International Champion Jay's Speedy Gonzales was a Best in Show winner and the #1 Chihuahua for 1971. Champion Gindon Bo Jangles is another on the list.

ne's TUSCARORA.

irmed A.K.C. Ch 12 June 76.

Can. and Am. Ch. Shillmaine's Tuscarora, confirmed champion as a puppy by Canadian Kennel Club in 1975; by American Kennel Club the following year. Winners Dog at Westminster in 1976. Owned by Shillmaine Chihuahuas, Capt. A.M.W. Samuels, Toronto, Canada.

Chapter 5

Chihuahuas in Canada

Our friends in Canada include numerous Chihuahua enthusiasts, making it clear that, as is the case wherever they are known, Chihuahuas have succeeded in capturing hearts there. The popularity of these little dogs, although especially notable in Ontario, is apparent in the other provinces, too, and they are making names for themselves from coast to coast.

As long ago as 1950 several breeders were getting under way, including Edna St. Hilaire, Ellen Overby, Sandra Nelles Edwards, and Judith Finch to name a few. After owning the breed as pets for awhile, interest in breeding and showing was aroused, and it might be said that the decade of the 1960s really started Chihuahuas forging ahead in the show ring.

In British Columbia, Edna St. Hilaire started with a Smooth puppy from Tressa Thurmer's kennel in the States who became Champion Hilaire's Jena Cherie. Owner-handled, this bitch became the #1 Smooth Chihuahua in Canada for 1968, and the "grand matriarch" behind a number of generations of descendants who have followed in her footsteps by also becoming #1 Smooth in their successive years of competition.

Ellen Overby, Tris-Tan Kennels, originally from Winnipeg in Manitoba, moved to Komaka, Ontario. Her first big winner, Canadian, American, and Mexican Champion Tris-Tan's Fascination, gained Canadian title in 1963. Now Tris-Tan Chihuahuas are known and respected worldwide, with representatives from there having contributed to breed progress in Africa, European countries, and elsewhere around the globe.

Sandra Nelles Edwards, who owns Brecon Kennels in Gormley, Ontario, since finishing her first in 1963, Champion Mae's Wee Pixie, (who went on to become Canada's Top Winning Chihuahua in 1964) has owned the Top Chihuahua on many occasions over the years. Added to this distinction has been the owning of in the area of a hundred Canadian champions, several dozen with American titles, plus champions of Bermuda and Mexico as well. The "star" of this kennel has been Canadian, American, Bermudian, Mexican, and F.C.I. Champion Brecon's Individualist, a home-bred who is a multiple Toy Group winner and has Specialty Show successes, having won these events in America on three occasions, plus a Westminster Best of Variety (1966) to his credit. This dog is famed as a sire as well as for his show ring successes, numbering among his progeny Betty Peterson's and Carol Humphrey's famous Best in Show winner, American, Canadian, and Mexican Champion Quantico's Little Crusader.

Individualist has sired a total of somewhere around 20 champions.

Another fancier whose Chihuahua activities got under way in the 1960s, Jean Westwood, Wisherwood Kennels, Victoria, British Columbia, breeds Long Coats as well as Smooths, having added the former in 1968, three years after getting going with the Smooths. Here the latter are based on Thurmer bloodlines from the United States, Brecon Kennels from Canada, and England's noted Kaitonias. The Longs are of Rayal breeding from California. American, Canadian, and Bermudian Champion Wisherwood El Tiro Del Tiger was 1977's Canadian Top Chihuahua.

On the following pages we bring you more about Canadian Chihuahua kennels and their winning dogs. These fanciers show quite regularly in the United States as well as at home and I have been impressed with the quality of those I have seen both on Canadian judging assignments and when they have come to the States for competition.

Am. and Can. Ch. Bridges Ardita Del Chillmaine. Canada's #3 Short Coat Chihuahua in 1982; #2 Short Coat Chihuahua in Canada in 1984. Has earned two legs to date on a Canadian C.D. along with many breed and Group honors in Canada and in the U.S. Owned and exclusively handled by Capt. A.M.W. Samuels, Shillmaine Kennels, Toronto, Ontario.

Ch. Hibou Petit D'Argent with handler Sue Rempel just after winning a Toy Group placement at Parkland Kennel Club for Heldon Chihuahuas, Donald and Mrs. Helen Hunt.

HELDON

Heldon Chihuahuas at Manitoba, are owned by Mrs. Helen Hunt and her son Don, and came about as a result of Don's wanting a hobby to enjoy. This young man was handicapped, having had cerebral palsy which he overcame to a large extent by pure determination. He made his living as a truck driver but wanted an interest for recreation. Since he was unable to participate in active sports, as his brother did, Don decided that he would like to show and breed dogs. He had friends who did so and who gave him some good advice when he was starting out: that the best way to get a really top winner was to breed it, as others who, when they produced something outstanding, were usually loathe to part with it.

So Don started looking for a female Chihuahua who might be suitable for his purposes. When an interesting brood bitch was advertised, he went to see her and came home with her, Lady Sandy. At first this bitch did not seem too promising, looking thin and with a very rough coat. Don's mother suggested that her son have a vet examine his new purchase, which he did, coming home with the word that the vet had told him she just needed time, lots of good food, and care. Under this routine Lady Sandy seemed to flourish, to the extent that even her breeder failed to recognize her when she saw the bitch after Don had owned it for awhile.

Next, Don looked for a suitable stud dog. Finding one he liked, he made arrangements immediately for Lady to be bred to him when ready, with the result that Lady and this dog produced a beautiful litter of three males and a female. They were all nice puppies, but Don decided that he would like to keep and show the female. You can call it beginner's luck or whatever, but in a very short time this puppy had become Champion Wee Tinker Belle. When the time came for her to be bred, Don sent her out to Timmy True of Tris-Tan. Tinker Belle had two pups this time, a male and a female. Again Don kept the female, Thumbelina, who truly loved every moment of every dog show. She was a real doll, weighing two-and-a-half to three pounds. Don showed her across Western Canada, where she attained many good Best of Variety wins and Group placements.

In her next litter Tinker Belle had three puppies, two female and one male, all of whom became champions. Champion Wee Princess Tanya was a black and tan very showy little dog and she became the dam of Champion Hibou Petit D'Argent who has sired some beautiful dogs. Also in this litter, She-Na-Na, the other golden tan female, has had several excellent puppies, among them Champion Heldon's Princess Naomi, Champion Heldon's Princess Nina D'Oro, and Heldon's Princess Juanita.

Champion Tris-Tan's Peter Pan was the Hunts' first stud dog. He was dark chocolate tan with an almost perfect head. He went Group 1st the second time he was in the ring, and was a champion before reaching seven months old. Additionally he was a splendid sire, his offspring including Champion Heldon Petit D'Argent. Another was Heldon's Honey Bee, whose litters are proving to be outstanding.

The Hunts have followed the policy of not keeping their stud dogs too long in order to avoid slipping into too close a type of in-breeding. Champion Heldon's El Campeador, full brother and littermate to Princess Naomi, the Top Winning Chihuahua Smooth Coat in Canada in 1984, is producing some very nice puppies.

When Don learned that he had a very short time left to live, he decided he wanted to continue showing his dogs as long as he was able. In September 1978, Don and Helen attended a seminar in Brandon conducted by Dr. Quentin LaHam. When Dr. LaHam saw Champion Blue Star Dust, a dark blue male Don had taken to the seminar, he said, "That's the finest Chihuahua I've ever seen." Blue's appearance was so outstanding that it created quite a sensation at that seminar and the two following dog shows. For some time afterward, Brandon residents visiting Winnipeg turned up at the Hunts' home wanting to see Blue. In Don's last days, Blue and Thumbelina were constantly with him. Later, Blue developed a heart condition and he died in October 1984. The memory of this marvelous little dog will always be alive in the thoughts of those who knew and loved him. Mrs. Hunt is especially happy that they now have a litter of his great-grandchildren who look especially promising.

The last shows Don attended with his dogs were the Metropolitan Shows in Toronto and the Kitchener-Waterloo shows. Shortly thereafter their return home he died. Mrs. Hunt comments, "Don was always grateful to the kind dog show people who gave him so much help and good advice, e.g., Mr. and Mrs. J. R. McDonald, George Polley, Ed Henderson, and many others."

Before Don's death of lung cancer, his mother promised him she would keep his dogs whom he loved so dearly, and continue showing them for him, which she has tried to do. About that same time her husband became legally blind and was unable to drive, and as Mrs. Hunt does not herself drive, this presented rather a problem. Therefore Mrs. Hunt has sent the dogs out with Sue Rempel, for whom they are continuing to do well. Mrs. Hunt is very happy and appreciative of this arrangment. We know that Don would be too!

A star of the future, Heldon's Wee Dinah Dee with nine points, winning Best Hound Puppy. Sue Rempel handling for Heldon Chihuahuas.

SHILLMAINE

Shillmaine Chihuahuas are owned by Captain A. M. W. Samuels at Mimico, Toronto, Ontario. Captain Samuels and his wife, Maureen (she is the one who does most of the breeding of the dogs) have been raising Chihuahuas since 1953, and Captain Andrews has been showing them in the States and Canada with notable success since about 1958.

Shillmaine Chihuahuas have as their foundation a good deal of Shroyer bloodlines. Their own Shillmaine winners by now trace back some half dozen generations at least—such well-known ones as Canadian and American Champion Shillmaine's Black Boozer, Canadian and American C.D.; and Canadian Champion Aztec Patilla Del Shillmaine and Canadian Champion Wee-Mite's Chiru of Shillmaine, to mention just a few, in the fifth generation behind some of the dogs born in the mid-1970's.

Some of the dogs owned by Captain and/or Mrs. Samuels who have met with spectacular success include the following:

Champion Shillmaine's Tiny Honey, Canadian and American C.D., completed his Canadian championship while still a puppy in 1960, to which a Canadian C.D. was added in 1961. He then added an American C.D. degree later in '61. He was owned and bred by Mrs. Maureen Samuels.

American and Canadian Champion Shillmaine's Pocohontas was bred by Mrs. Samuels and owned by the Captain. She became a Canadian Champion in 1964, then an American Champion three years later. As a show bitch she was highly successful, and was Canada's #2 Chihuahua in 1964, #3 in 1965. Her wins in the States included a Group 2nd and also she was Best of Winners at Westminster in 1965.

One of the most exciting of the Samuels's Chihuahuas was the truly great little American and Canadian Champion Shillmaine's Vivita Plata, again owned by the Captain and bred by Mrs. Maureen Samuels, born in September 1969. She was by Floray's Toyah Dell Shillmaine ex Mamita (daughter of Champion Shroyer Elkatawa Shillmaine).

Vivita was a Canadian Champion in 1970, an American Champion in 1972, her points for the latter having been earned with four majors. She was Best of Opposite Sex at Westminster Kennel Club, and, when Captain Samuels decided to campaign her a bit more extensively in the United States, she gained an impressive

Can. and Am. Ch. Shillmaine's Pocohontas, Canada's #2 Chihuahua in 1964 and #3 in 1965, Best of Winners at Westminster in 1965, also had Group placements in both countries.

number of Best of Variety wins. In Canada she has many enviable wins, including a Group placement at ten years' age.

Canadian and American Champion Shillmaine's Tuscarora, owned and bred by Mrs. Maureen Samuels, was born in October 1974, a son of Canadian Champion Shroyer Elkatawa Shillmaine (who sired four American Champions and one Canadian Champion) ex Linterna De Oro (an Elkatawa daughter).

Tuscarora was a Canadian Champion as a puppy in 1975, gained American Kennel Club Championship in 1976, and was Winners Dog at Westminster in 1976.

Currently the Shillmaine banner is being kept high by American and Canadian Champion Bridges Ardita Del Shillmaine, a chocolate and tan female born in January 1979 by Poo-Chi-Dal's Pat of Bobbieann (Champion Luce's Ima Smarty ex Champion Northern

Desert of Bobbie Ann) from Bridges Parkline Vargo's Miss (Varga's Parkline Blue Moon ex Parkline Horsie). Ardita was bred by Shirley and Robert Bridges and has some 80 Group placements between the United States and Canada and, as a show dog, was Canada's #3 Chihuahua in 1982 and #2 in 1984. Additionally, Ardita is one of Captain Samuels's Obedience stars having two legs, as we write this, on her Canadian C.D. degree after which she will start work on a C.D. degree in the United States.

Obedience has always been important to Captain Samuels, and he has four Chihuahuas with Dual C.D. degrees, i.e., dogs who have earned this distinction in both the United States and Canada. Probably his most famed of these so far is Shillmaine's ity orang, Canadian and American C.D., whose degree in Canada was earned

Two noted winning Chihuahuas from Canada's famous Shillmaine Kennels owned by Capt. A.M.W. Samuels.

Ch. Vivila Plata

Can. and Am.

1st. in Gp. 5 1970

Ch. Sacajawea

Can. and Am.

1st. in Gp. 5 1969

Ch. Shillmaine's Tiny Honey, Am. and Can. C.D., was an important show and obedience winner around 1960, having gained his Canadian bench show title that year, followed by his Canadian C.D. in May of that year and his American C.D. the following November. Owned and bred by Mrs. Maureen Samuels, Shillmaine Chihuahuas.

with scores of 192, 175½, and 190, having been completed in September 1984. In America during 1984 he was Highest Scoring Toy in Novice B. This little dog is a son of Champion Shillmaine's Arapaho, American and Canadian C.D.

An interesting note on Shillmaine's ity orang is that he was named in the Malayan language in which case this should not be spelled with capital letters. It translates "of the man" and "iti" is pronounced "itu."

Captain Samuels tells us that finally, in 1984 after a number of years working toward this end, he has been successful in persuading the Canadian Kennel Club to include the type of coat (i.e., Long Coat or Short Coat) on Chihuahua registration certificates, thus enabling breeders who wish to do so to keep their lines purely of whichever coat type they have chosen rather than run the risk of interbreeding unknowingly between the two.

Eng. Ch. Anyako Admiral, fawn/sable/white Long Coat dog, born in 1982, a homebred from the Anyako Kennels of Mrs. Hazel Mitchell, Moffat, Dumfriesshire, Scotland. Winner of five Challenge Certificates.

Chapter 6

Chihuahuas in Great Britain

It was during the 1940s when the noted British authority Mrs. Phyllis Robson, editor of the English *Dog World* magazine, during one of her annual trips to the United States told me that she had been asked to select some outstanding Chihuahuas for her friend, the talented English breeder Mrs. Thelma Gray whose Rozavel Kennel prefix was and still is as famous throughout the world of purebred dogs for her Beagles and Corgis, as it came to be for Chihuahuas. Mrs. Robson carefully covered the entire United States on this mission. Her tremendous knowledge of all breeds of dog was very well-known.

Mrs. Robson told me that up until that time there was little Chihuahua interest in Great Britain. Mrs. Gray, however, had seen and admired some good ones in her travels and was anxious to embark on a breeding program for them.

The success of this breeding program is indisputable. Dogs owned by Thelma Gray or of her breeding have gained prestigious honors at the great Crufts Dog Show and at other leading British events. Some years ago Mrs. Gray moved from England to Australia where she remained until her death a few years back. She had judged around the world, including Chihuahua Specialties in the United States, and did much to increase British interest in the breed.

The well-known Irish breeder Barbara Scott of Cornamona Chihuahuas at Dublin, Ireland, based her breeding program on Rozavel and has produced numerous homebred champions who have done credit to her and to their background.

The late Margaret Rider of Horley, Surrey, England, was another influential breeder of Chihuahuas. This is also true of Joan Forster.

There is a British Chihuahua Club active on behalf of the breed; and a Chihuahua Club of Ireland.

Now to tell you a bit about some of the winning Chihuahuas of the present day in Great Britain.

ANYAKO

Anyako Chihuahuas, featuring both Long Coated and Smooth Coat varieties of Chihuahuas, were founded in 1961 by Mrs. Hazel E. Mitchell, Moffat, Dunfriesshire, Scotland. For the first 15 years, no stud dogs were kept there, but a strong, self-whelping bitch line was established, based largely on Rozavel bloodlines. Since the mid-1970s, both dogs and bitches have been kept and campaigned in the show ring. Winners bred by Mrs. Mitchell include, in the home team, Champion Anyako Airborne, S/C and Champion Anyako Admiral, L/C; and in other ownership, Knockenjig Anyako Lone Star, L/C; Champion Molomor Anyako Astronaut, S/C; Champion Apoco Deodar Anyako Hill Billy, L/C; Australian Champion Rozavel Anyako Avenger, S/C; and South African Champion Anyako Desperate Dan of Bridgepost, S/C.

Champion Anyako Airborne was sired by Champion Molomor Anyako Astronaut ex Anyako Tosca, both parents having been sired by Champion Rozavel Chief Scout. A dog with five Challenge Certificates to his credit, he is still an outstanding example of the breed at nine years of age.

Champion Anyako Bandmaster was sired by Champion Apoco Deodar Music Man ex Anyako Wandering Star (by Champion Winterlea Lone Wolf, a son of Champion Rozavel Wolf Cub.) Bandmaster's record of ten Challenge Certificates is an imposing one. He was born in September 1977, bred and owned by Mrs. Hazel Mitchell.

Eng. Ch. Anyako Airborne, blue fawn Smooth Coat dog, born in July 1976. A homebred owned by Mrs. Hazel Mitchell, Annan Water Schoolhouse, Moffat, Scotland. Winner of five Challenge Certificates, fit and sound today at age nine years.

Eng. Ch. Anyako Bandmaster, fawn-sable Long Coat dog born September 1977. Outstanding winner of 10 Challenge Certificates, this is another outstanding homebred from the Anyako Kennels of Mrs. Hazel Mitchell. Photo by J.K. and E.A. McFarlane, Wakefield, W. Yorks.

Champion Anyako Admiral is another homebred Long Coat and also a consistent winner of Challenge Certificates in keenest competition—a homebred son of Champion Molomor Adastro (by Champion Molomor Anyako Astronaut ex Anyako Tiggy Winkle (litter sister to Champion Anyako Bandmaster).

DOLANDI

Dolandi Chihuahuas are owned and shown by Diana and Laurence Fitt-Savage, Sandringham, Norfolk, England, who also are leading breeders of Japanese Chin.

English Champion Dolandi Godolphinsson has brought much fame to this kennel as a Challenge Certificate and Best of Breed winner at prestigious shows, and is, as well, the sire of champions and other winners.

Champion Dolandi Bobble is an exquisite Long Coat bitch by Dolandi Godolphin ex Widogi Blaise (thus a double granddaughter of the tremendously influential sire in Long Coats during the 1970s and early 1980s, English Champion Widogi Playboy). Bobble's show successes include Junior Warrant winner and Challenge Certificate at British Chihuahua Club November 1978, judge Mrs. H. M. Enders; Crufts 1980, Mr. R. J. Clay; and Manchester 1980, Mr. J. Currie. Reserve Challenge Certificates were awarded her by Mrs. B. Currie, Mrs. C. Robinson, and Mrs. P. Cross-Stern.

Dolandi King Swinger, born January 1982, is a Long Coat dog by Champion Dolandi Godolphinsson ex Dolandi Harmony Bell, and is a consistent winner at important shows.

Dolandi Victor Ludorum, Smooth Coat dog by Dolandi Oliver ex Dolandi Rise and Shine, is a Junior Warrant winner who won his first seven classes but, since an unpleasant experience at a show, has come to dislike both the shows themselves and travelling. Truly a pity!

Dolandi Petite Fleur, Long Coat, who won Reserve C.C. at Ulster Chihuahua Club under Mrs. S. Stevenson, and Dolandi Josephine who was Best Smooth Coat bitch at the Chihuahua Club of South Wales under judge Herr G. Julenius from Sweden, were out of the ring owing to maternal duties during much of 1984.

EILEEN LUCAS

Eileen Lucas of Mansfield, Notts., England, is a devoted fan-

Eng. Ch. Dolandi Bobble, Long Coat female born May 1977 by Dolandi Godolphin ex Widogi Modesty Blaise, both parents sired by the highly influential sire, Eng. Ch. Widogi Playboy. Owned by Diana and Laurence Fitt-Savage, Dolandi Chihauhaus, Sandringham, Norfolk.

Dolandi King Swinger (*left*) red sable Long Coat born January 1982; and, Dolandi Victor Ludorum (*right*), cream Smooth Coat, born November 1981. Both from the Dolandi Kennels.

cier of the Chihuahua and the owner of the very lovely bitch Eladrew's Polly Flinders.

Polly was bred by Mrs. Elaine Gunn and came to live with Ms. Lucas at age eight months. She began her show career at 11 months, winning two first prizes and Best of Breed at her very first Open Show. Since then she has won her way through all of her classes and is now restricted to open class competition at Championship Shows only.

At Open and Championship events, Polly has won 34 first prizes, Best Puppy Bitch at the Long Coat Chihuahua Club Specialty, four reserve Challenge Certificates, and her first Challenge Certificate, plus 16 Bests of Breed at Open Shows.

Polly's sire is English Champion Glaisdaleast Joshua of Sandavo (by Champion Widogi Playboy, a son of Champion Molomor Anyaka Astronaut), her dam being Eladrew's Bo-Peep, daughter of Champion Dolandi Godolphinsson. On both sides, her pedigree goes back to Rozavel with a number of Thelma Grey's best known dogs represented.

English Champion Glaisdaleast Joshua of SanDavo, Polly's sire, was owned by Mrs. V. Gillott and is known as one of England's leading Chihuahua producers. He is a son of Champion Widogi Playboy who was owned by Mrs. J. Fraser until his death in 1984 at 13 years of age. He, too, was one of the top sires in England. Polly's grandsire is also a grandson of Champion Widogi Playboy and he is owned by Mrs. Fitt-Savage.

1 ▲ 2 ▼

← **Overleaf:**

1. Ch. Mignon's Becky Duvall, lovely Long Coat owned by Mignon Murray, Jacksonville, Florida.

2. Ch. Apoco Deodar Best Suit, by Apoco Deodar Aristocrat ex Apoco Deodar Domino was bred by Bill and Sylvia Stevenson and is owned by Mary M. Silkworth, Jackson, Michigan. Handled by Peter Green, this handsome little dog has numerous outstanding wins to his credit, among them Best of Variety Long Coat at the 1985 National Specialty. He is an English import, was born in 1981, and when he left England had accounted for a total of 22 Challenge Certificates there.

Overleaf: →

1. Brite Star Polaris of Shroyer, the foundation bitch of Brite Star Chihuahuas, has 12 points including a 5-point major; is a Top Champion Producer; and a Multiple Winner of Best Brood Bitch in Specialty Shows. Owned by Ms. Elizabeth Bickel, Kansas City, Missouri.

2. Brite Star Orion, C.D., Obedience *Dog World* award winner. Tied for 1st place in his Novice Division at the A.K.C. Centennial 1984. High Scoring Chihuahua, A.K.C. Centennial with 197½. This handsome Long Coat is #1 Obedience Ranked Chihuahua for 1985. Ms. Elizabeth Bickel, owner, Kansas City, Missouri.

3. Ch. Tiny Mite's Tag-a-Long, by Ch. Tiny Mite's Terrific ex Tiny Mite's Valentine, finished with a 3 and 5 point majors, all Specialty wins. Here taking Winners Dog for 5 points, Best Puppy in Show and Best Bred-by-Exhibitor in Show, age seven months, at Chihuahua Club of Michigan, November 1982. Owned by Robert L. DeJonge, handled by Helen DeJonge, Tiny Mite Chihuahuas, Zeeland, Michigan.

4. Ch. Flint's Lil Sunny Boy Robin, bred and owned by Robert and Patsy Flint, Dayton, Ohio, taking Best of Winners at Dayton K.C. in 1982. Jim Lehman handling this handsome Long Coat.

5. Kimball's Playboy of Dugger, owned by W.H. and G. Kimball, taking Winners Dog from the author at Chihuahua Club of Atlanta Specialty on April 10, 1980.

6. Ch. Komo's Tao Mya Cheta Tatoo taking the second of four majors, breeder/owner/-handled by Katherine J. Hood, later owned by Mrs. Lloyd Reeves, Georgetown, Florida. The show, Glens Falls K.C. in 1982. The judge Joe Rowe. Cheta is by Ch. Komo's Tao Yankee Skipper ex Komo's Tao TSP of Sugar.

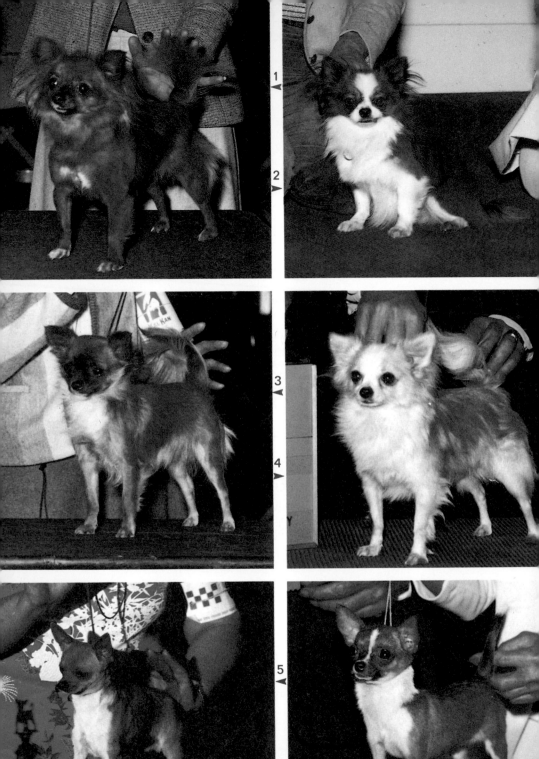

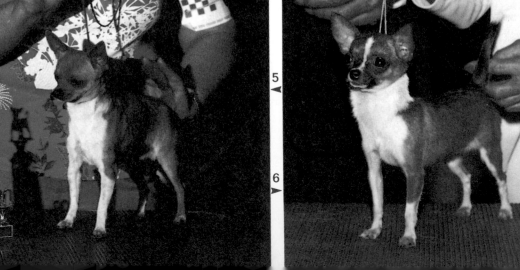

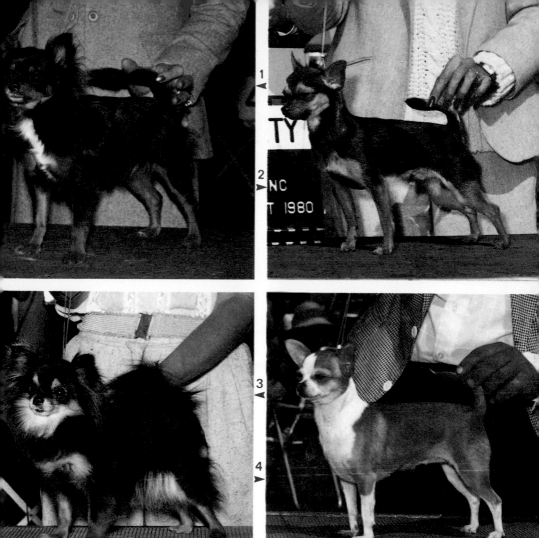

1 ▶

2 ▶ NC
T 1980

3 ▶

4 ▶

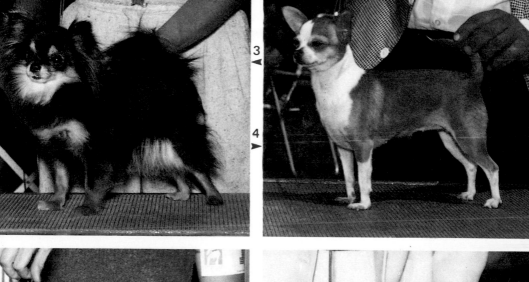

5 ▶

6 ▶

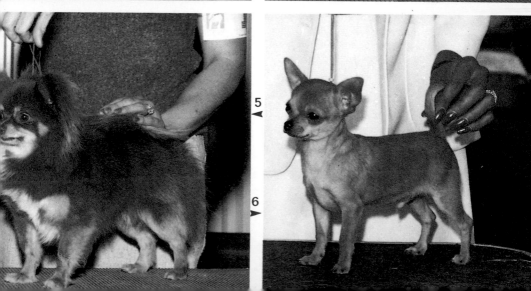

← Overleaf:

1. Ch. Brite Star Summer Night, Long Coat, taking Best of Winners and Best of Opposite Sex at Chihuahua Club of Maryland Specialty in 1981. This Long Coat was also Best of Winners at the Chihuahua Club of Greater New York. Brite Star Chihuahuas are owned by Ms. Elizabeth Bickel, Kansas City, Missouri.

2. Harmony's Sounder of Weseleyan, Smooth Coat dog taking Best of Variety at Ramapo Kennel Club 1980. Owner-handled by Linda Glenn, Glindale Chihuahuas, Harrington Park, New Jersey.

3. Ch. Brite Star Black Velvet Night, Long Coat, is the newest Brite Star Champion for 1985. Ms. Elizabeth Bickel, owner, Kansas City, Missouri.

4. Harmony's Hugabee of Glindale, handled by David Harmon for owner Linda M. Glenn, Harrington Park, New Jersey. Here taking Best of Variety at Newton K.C. in 1980.

5. Ch. Brite Star Galactic Firework, Long Coat, taking Winners Dog at the 1984 Houston Chihuahua Club Specialty. Pictured finishing with his third major. Ms. Elizabeth Bickel, owner, Kansas City, Missouri.

6. Ch. Glindale's Mighty Munchkin, born March 1981, by Garrowglen's Ay Fonz of Dunbar ex Harmony's Bugbe Rigs O'Glindale, at age six months taking Reserve Winners at Westchester Kennel Club. Owned by Linda and Joseph M. Glenn, Harrington Park, New Jersey.

1. This lovely headstudy is of the noted English winning Long Coat Chihuahua, Eladrew's Polly Flinders, by Eng. Ch. Glaisdaleast Joshua of Sandavo. Owned by Eileen Lucas, Mansfield, Notts, England.

2. Okatoma's Mr. Cool, C.D.X., Ch. Okatoma's Lickedy Split, and Pete's Whiskey Lady C.D. (Lickedy Split's mother) are all owned by Patricia Lambert, Hattiesburg, Mississippi.

3. *Dog World* award winner, Brite Star Orion, C.D., retrieving over the high jump in practice for his C.D.X. Ms. Elizabeth Bickel, owner, Kansas City, Missouri.

4. Ch. Mooney's SuCie Miclanjo, born March 1972, at the Chihuahua Club of America National Specialty in October 1984 in Chicago, where she was awarded first prize over a large entry and one of the very first Hill's Science Diet Senior Awards. SuCie also in 1984 was Best Long Coat Veteran at the Chihuahua Club of America National In Maryland and Best Veteran in Show at the host Club for that week-end, the Chihuahua Club of Maryland Specialty. The judges Dr. William Field and Dr. T. Allen Kirk, respectively.

5. Two-month-old Chihuahuas owned by Shinybrook Kennels illustrating the importance of early show training. They are by Shinybrook Heart Throb ex Shinybrook Tillitu.

6. More Dolandi Chihuahuas at play. Owned by Diana and Laurence Fitt-Savage, Sandringham, Norfolk, England.

7. JP's Pequena Rambo, *left,* and JP's Pequena Rita, *right,* as puppies. Two adorable Chihuahua "charmers" from the JP Kennels owned by Judy Padgug, Sacramento, California.

8. Schroder's Huggybear De JP obedience training to "heel." Owned by Judy Padgug, JP Chihuahuas, Sacramento, California.

1
2
3
4
5
6
7
8

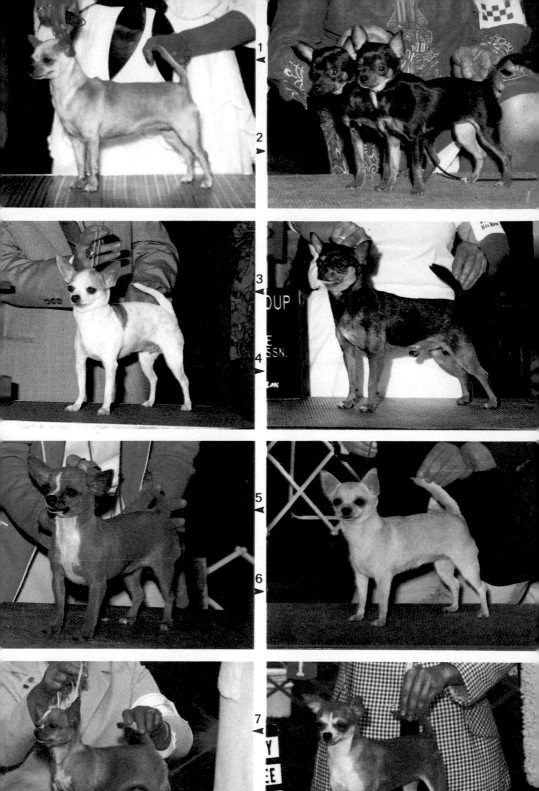

← Overleaf:

1. Ch. Heldon's Princess Naomi, Top Winning Smooth Coat Chihuahua in Canada 1984, was bred by Donald Hunt, co-owner with his mother, Helen Hunt, of Heldon Chihuahuas, Winnipeg, Manitoba. Sue Rempel handled.

2. Ch. Holiday's Hotcha and littermate, by Ch. Holiday's Hershey Bar ex Holiday's Blue Saphire D'Oro, bred by Mary Myers, Holiday Chihuahuas, Phoenix, Arizona. At six months' age winning Best Brace in Toy Group at Lake Shore K.C. in 1979.

3. Ch. H and J's Crystal Princess going Best of Opposite Sex at the National Chihuahua Specialty in Chicago in 1984. Jack Phariss handled under judge Dorothy Welsh. H and J Chihuahuas, Bryan, Texas.

4. Ch. Pittore's Saber Dancer winning Best Toy at Jacksonville K.C. in May 1982. Handled by Joyce McComiskey for Patricia Pittore, Goshen, Massachusetts.

5. This handsome Smooth dog by Komo's Tao Cameron Corino ex Komo's Tao Cantabella is Ch. Komo's Tao C.C. Castinetta. Bred, owned, and handled by Katherine J. Hood, Komo Chihuahuas. The new owner is Mrs. Lloyd Reeves, S. Woodstock, Vermont.

6. Ch. Dartan's Saree So Sweet, by Ch. Dartan's Pirate Blackbeard ex Dartan's Connie, winning one of two Toy Groups from the classes on the way to her title. Handled by breeder-owner Darwin Delaney in this picture at Greater Muskegon in August 1984. Owned by Darwin and Tanya Delaney, Dartan Chihuahuas, Essexville, Michigan.

7. Ch. Call's Delightful Design winning one of her many Toy Group 1sts at Evergreen, Colorado. Handled as always by breeder-owner Annie D. Call, Kaysville, Utah.

8. Ch. Dartan Dominique D'Quachitah taking Best of Variety at the Milwaukee Specialty. Handled by owner, Linda George. Dominique was Best in Show on July 25, 1981 at Waukesha, Wisconsin, under Mrs. Jane Kay. Since then Dominique has been owned by breeders Darwin and Tanya Delaney. She is a daughter of Ch. Quachitah Apocalypse ex Ch. Dartan's Calamity Jane.

Overleaf: ⟶

1. Ch. Call's The Tawnee Tutone, by Quantico's Little Crusader ex Call's Little Penny Princess. Owned and handled by Chester P. or Annie D. Call, Kaysville, Utah.

2. Ch. Flint's Carbon Copy Robin, by Ch. Flint's Lil Lucky Robin ex Ch. Flint's Pretty Fancy Robin, a noted Toy Group winning and placing Long Coat bred and owned by Robert and Patsy Flint, Dayton, Ohio. Handled by Jim Lehman.

3. Patricia Lambert, Okatoma Chihuahuas, Hattiesburg, Mississippi, with some of "the family." *Left* to *right,* Middy, Ch. Skeeter, Whiskey C.D., Fonzie C.D.X., and Ch. Classy.

4. Ch. Bayard Belle of the Ball, by Ch. RJR Reginald of Bayard ex Ch. Bayard I Love Lucy of Alvin, homebred owned by Melanie Newell, Cambridge, Maryland.

5. Although noted primarily for outstanding Smooths, Pittore Chihuahuas have done their share with the Long Coats, too. Here is Xochipilli winning a Best in Show in Mexico. This little dog is also an American Champion that was bred by Pat Pittore and is owned by Mr. Alonso in Mexico. Sired by Pittore's Dickey Bear of Oz (Champion Dickie Chip–Champion Pittore's Nedda of Oz) ex Pittore's Lavon Chip O'Sage (Champion Dickie Chip–Champion Pittore's Sage).

6. The very famous Long Coat Chihuahua, Ch. Round Table The One and Only, handled by Jordan L. Chamberlain for Round Table Kennels in an entry of 215 in Chicago in October 1978. Best of Breed was judged by the late Mrs. Thelma Gray, celebrated owner of the Rozavel kennels in England and Australia.

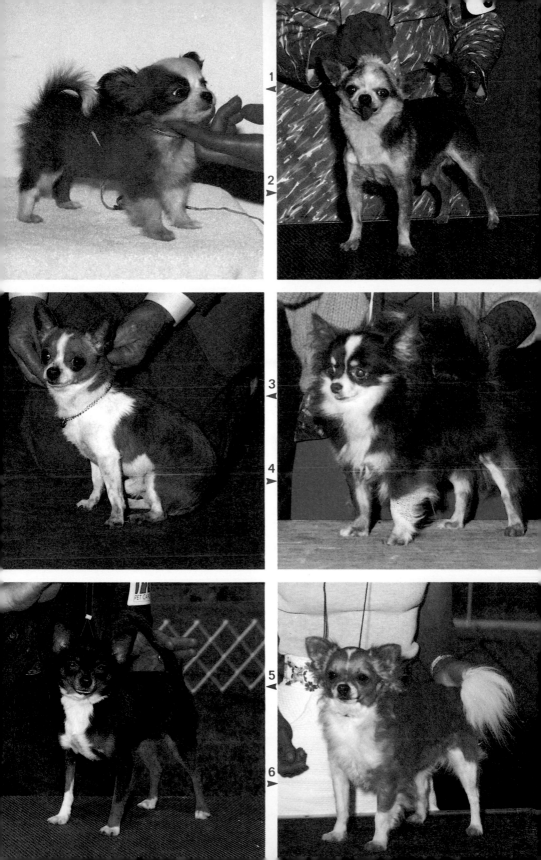

← Overleaf:

1. Show training should start at a very early age. This is 12-week-old Brite Star Twinkle learning how to pose nicely. Ms. Elizabeth Bickel, owner, Kansas City, Missouri.

2. Ch. Varga's Richardo De Oro, by Sochor's Freddy ex Varga's Hello Dolly De Oro, born January 1971, winning the Veterans Class at the Dallas Specialty, March 1981. Bred by Edith Vargo. Owned and handled by Mary Myers, Holiday Chihuahuas, Phoenix, Arizona. Richardo is the sire of several champions.

3. Shillmaine's iti orang, Can. and Am. C.D., is a well-known obedience "star" in both countries. This is the fourth of his owner's Dual Champions, and he is sired by Ch. Shillmaine's Arapaho, Can. and Am. C.D. Note that this little dog is named in the Malayan language, and therefore correctly the name is not capitalized. Owned by Captain A.M.W. Samuels, Shillmaine Chihuahuas, Mimico, Toronto, Canada.

4. Ch. Komo's Tao Monte Rey Rayo is owned and handled by Katherine J. Hood, Komo's Chihuahuas and Art Studio, Altamont, Illinois. Here shown winning Best Long Coat at Roanoke K.C. in 1979.

5. Ch. Lazy VK Caroline Miclanjo, by Ch. Tiny Mite's McDuff ex Ch. Lazy VK Torkina, finished her title on her 14-month birthday with four majors. She is pictured placing Toy Group 4th her first time out as a special. Bred by Kathleen Brown and Michael P. Mooney, co-owned by Ms. Brown and Carolyn A. Mooney.

6. Long Coat Chihuahua, Am. and Can. Ch. Terrymont Marsubri Toto Ruff, Am. and Can. U.D. was bred by Terrymont Kennels and Marcia Greenburg, Suffield, Connecticut. A very distinguished show and obedience winner owned by Susan Fischer Payne, Suffield, Connecticut.

1. Best in Show winner Ch. Holiday's Tijuana La Cune. This stunning little dog is the result of a Smooth and Long Coat breeding, and was #1 Smooth Coat bitch and #2 Smooth Coat Chihuahua for 1980. Bred and owned by Mary Myers, Holiday Chihuahuas, Phoenix, Arizona.

2. Chihuahuas are great for young handlers, being a manageable size and bright, alert little dogs. Here is Peggy Myers, grandaughter of Mrs. Mary Myers, just after beating Grandma for the prize. Mrs. Myers had told Peggy to "hang on to him good while on the table," and Peggy clearly was obeying the directions. This little dog is Ch. Holiday's Ink Spot De Oro, sired by Ch. Holiday's Spot Silver ex Holiday's Ritzie De Oro. Bred and owned by Mary Myers, Holiday Chihuahuas, Phoenix, Arizona.

3. Ch. Eric's C.P. Chip of Oz, by Ch. Eric's Joe Louie of Oz, with co-breeder/owner Annette Mellinger.

4. Glindale's Tru Blue Sam photographed in a sugar bowl by John Ashbey. Owner, Linda M. Glenn, Glindale Chihuahuas, Harrington Park, New Jersey.

← Overleaf:

1. Brite Star's foundation English import. Glaisdaleast Fantasia, C.D.X., is behind some of the leading winners from this kennel. Owned by Ms. Elizabeth Bickel, Kansas City, Missouri.

2. Ch. Goldenbay's Moonglow of Hack's Pack, by Best in Show winning Ch. Elh Mighty Lunar of Darton ex Ch. Hack's Pack Velvet Imp, grew up to become famous. Owned by Pat Porreca, Pleasanton, California.

3.. Mother and son! Brite Star Andromeda and Ch. Brite Star Little Dipper are owned by Ms. Elizabeth Bickel, Kansas City, Missouri. Note that these two are perched on the head of a friend!

4. Linda M. Glenn with two of her favorite Chihuahuas, Ch. Glindale's Mighty Munchkin and Glindale's Itty Bitty 8-Ball. Glindale Chihuahuas, Harrington Park, New Jersey. Photo by Herbert Horowitz.

1. Ch. Dugger's Black Imp finished title in August 1980. Pat Porreca, owner, Golden Bay Chihuahuas, Pleasanton, California.

2. Ch. Goldenbay's Moonglow of Hack's Pack taking points on the way to title at San Joaquin, June 1984. Owned by Pat Porreca, Pleasanton, California.

3. Ch. Flint's Mr. Mischief, by Ch. Flint's Carbon Robin ex Hardwerk's Missie Mischief, taking Best of Winners on the way to his title, handled by Jim Lehman for Robert and Patsy Flint, Dayton, Ohio.

4. Ch. Flint's Lucky Lady of Lunar, by Ch. Elh's Mighty Lunar of Dartan ex Flint's Lil Candy Rose Robin, one of the lovely Smooth Coats owned and bred by Flint, Dayton, Ohio. Handled by Jim Lehman.

5. Glindale's Pee Wee Power winning in Bermuda in 1982. Linda M. Glenn, Harrington Park, New Jersey.

6. Call's Happy Hooligan taking 4th in Toy Group at Intermountain Kennel Club, Salt Lake City, Utah, October 1978. Owned by Call's Chihuahuas, Chester P. and Annie D. Call, Kaysville, Utah.

7. Ch. Holiday's Tijuana Taxi, littermate to Best in Show winning Ch. Holiday's Tijuana La Cune, by Varga's Tijuana Midnite Sun ex Holiday's Hot Butterscotch, was bred and is owned by Mary Myers, Holiday Chihuahuas, Phoenix, Arizona. Handled on this occasion by John Myers.

8. Ch. Mignon's Pete's Pam at age 10 months. Owned by Mignon Murray, Jacksonville, Florida.

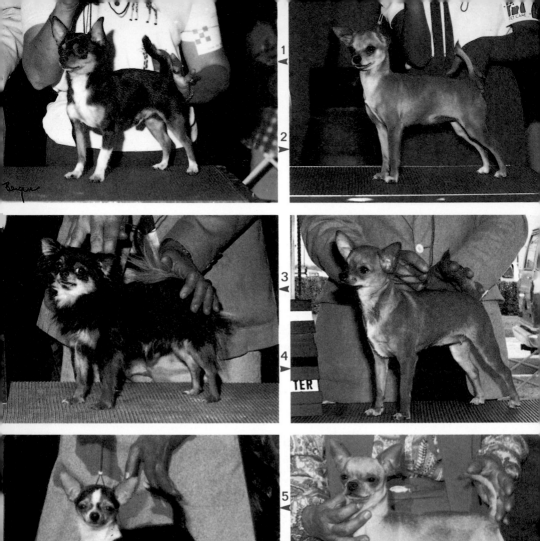

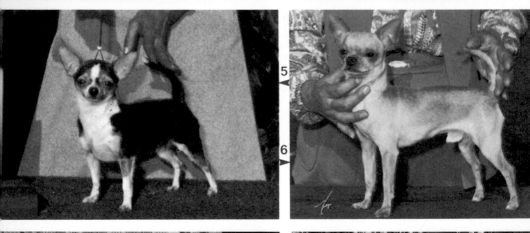

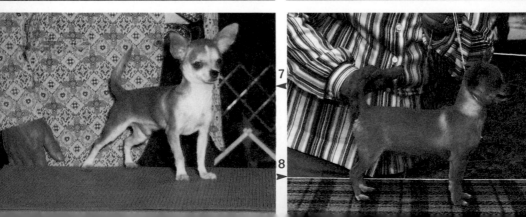

1

2

3

4

5

6

7

8

←—Overleaf:

1. Ch. Eric's Peter Munchkin, owned by Eric's "Oz" Chihuahuas, Annette, Dan and Eric J. Mellinger, Matawan, New Jersey. Handled by Mike Smith, Munchkin is taking Best of Variety at Sussex Hills K.C. in 1981.

2. As a class bitch, Ch. Eric's C.P. Chip of Oz, bred and owned by A. Mellinger and E. Mellinger, House of Oz, Matawan, New Jersey, is taking Best of Opposite Sex at Rockland County K.C. in March 1984. Owner-handled by Annette Mellinger.

3. Ch. Hurd's Marty, by Ch. Hurd's Ala Baba ex Ch. Hurd's Sweet Melissa, here is winning the Toy Group at Council Bluffs in May 1981. Also Best of Variety and Best of Opposite Sex to Best of Breed at Chihuahua Club of America Specialty Show. Marty was a grandson of Ch. Hurd's Kojak, a result of inter-breeding Hurd's Long Coat and Smooth Coat lines. Bred by Max E. Hurd. Handler and co-owner, Marie Hurd, Council Bluffs, Iowa.

4. The great Ch. Call's Delightful Desire scoring one of her numerous Toy Group victories.

5. Ch. Dartan's Barbary Coast, by Ch. Dartan's Pirate Blackbeard ex Dartan's Connie, was Winners Dog and Best of Winners at the Chihuahua Club of America Specialty his first time out, age seven months. Undefeated to his championship, he is now being "specialed." Also Best of Variety and Best of Opposite Sex to Best of Breed at the Chihuahua Club of America Specialty. Shown winning a Toy Group, 2nd, St. Joseph K.C., 1984. Bred by Darwin and Tanya Delaney. Owned and handled by Max E. Hurd.

6. Ch. Dartan's Tailor Made winning Best of Variety at the Toledo Kennel Club in June 1985 from the classes over seven specials on his way to Group 1st. The previous day had been Best Puppy in Sweepstakes at the Chihuahua Club of America Specialty. Sired by Dartan's Tuff E Nuff ex Bo Jangles Bobbyjean Dartan. Bred and owned by Darwin and Tanya Delaney, Dartan Chihuahuas, Essexville, Michigan. Mr. Delaney handled in this event.

7. Ch. Brite Star Galactic Magic taking Best of Opposite Sex to Best of Breed, Chihuahua Club of America week-end in Maryland. Owned by Brite Star Chihuahuas, Ms. Elizabeth Bickel, Kansas City, Missouri.

8. Ch. Darwin's Pirate Blackbeard winning Best of Breed, over a record entry of 277 dogs, at the Chihuahua Club of America National Specialty in 1984 under judge Dorothy Welsh. At the time of this picture, Pirate was owned by Russ and Joan Kruetzman. He is now owned by his breeders, Darwin and Tanya Delaney. Top Producing Sire of Chihuahuas for 1984, he has sired seven champion offspring. Pirate is also the sire of all-breed Best in Show winner Ch. Jo-El's Drummer Boy. Pirate was sired by Ch. Handwerk's Lucky Strike ex Dartan's Black Eyed Susan.

1. Ch. Tiny Mite's Terrific, by Buster Brown of Tiny Mite ex Ch. Clement's Captivating Cathy, is handled by Terri Lydden for owners, Tiny Mite Chihuahuas, Robert L. De-Jonge, Zeeland, Michigan.

2. Ch. Flint's Lil Precious Miracle, by Ch. Flint's Carbon Copy Robin ex Ch. Flint's Precious Jewel Robin, bred and owned by Robert and Patsy Flint, Dayton, Ohio. Taking a Group placement at Michigan K.C. in 1983. Handled by Jim Lehman.

3. Ch. Elh's Mighty Lunar of Dartan, seven times an all-breed Best in Show winner, here is winning Best in Show at the Golden Gate Kennel Club in 1984, under judge Roy Ayers. Handled by Mike Diaz. "Buddy" was owned by Ellinor Hasting and Marc and Sheila Peters at the time of this win. He is now owned by Pat and Bob Porreca. Bred by Darwin and Tanya Delaney, he was sired by Ch. Handwerk's Lucky Strike ex Dartan's Narona.

4. Ch. Dartan's Bristol Cream, multiple Specialty Best of Breed winner and Group winner during the early 1980s. Owned, bred and handled by Darwin and Tanya Delaney, Dartan Chihuahuas, Essexville, Michigan. Sired by Ch. Dartan's Super Dude ex Ch. Dartan's I Dream of Jeannie.

5. Ch. Flint's Ruff, Tuff 'n' Ready Robin was sired by Ch. Flint's Lucky Jeri Robin ex Handwerk's Big Bertha. Bred and owned by Robert and Patsy Flint, here taking Best of Winners. Handled by Jim Lehman.

6. Flint's Lil Joy of Jiri Robin going Winners Bitch at Western Reserve Kennel Club 1983. Jim Lehman handled for Robert and Patsy Flint, Dayton, Ohio.

7. This appealing and attractive Long Coat is Ch. How About Jason Chip, sired by Ch. Lucky's Dickie Chip of Oz ex Palmer's Elite Martie. Bred by Betty Bohrer, owned by Bohrer Kennels, Zionsville, Pennsylvania.

8. The great little Smooth Coat male, Ch. Quachitah For Your Eyes Only, winning Best in Show under Michele Billings at Toledo K.C. in June 1983. Bred, owned and handled by Linda George, Quachitah Chihuahuas, Waukesha, Wisconsin.

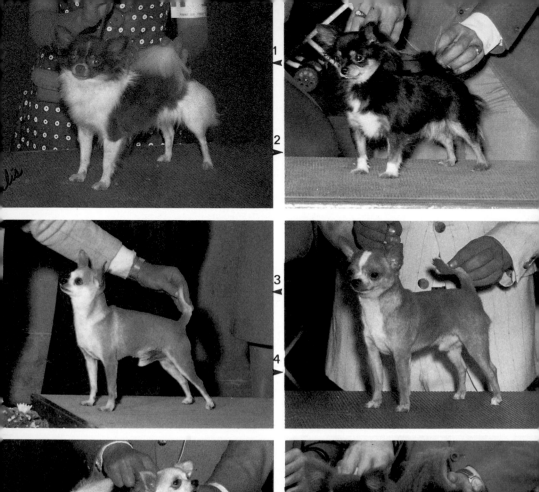

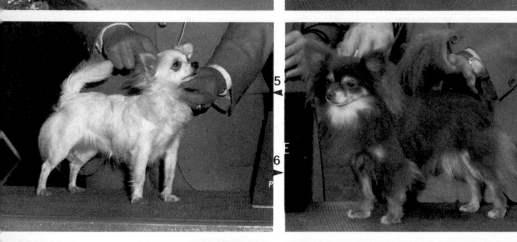

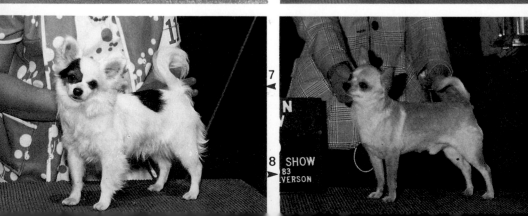

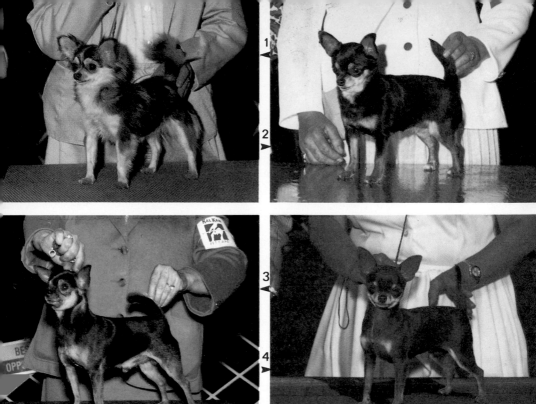

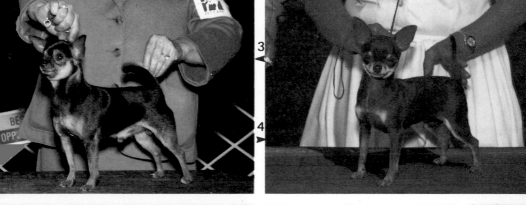

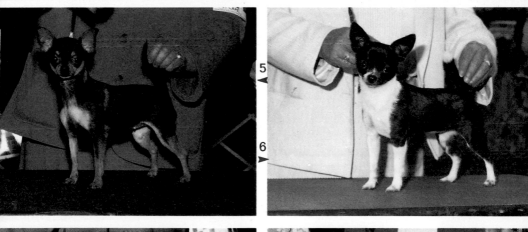

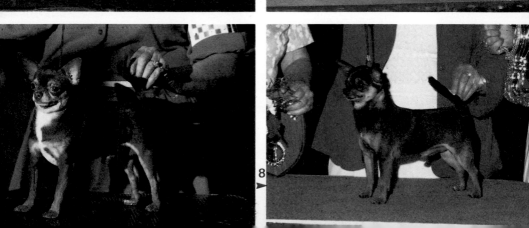

← **Overleaf:**

1. Ch. Miclanjo Kaleidoscope, by Ch. Miclanjo Wilhewag of Lazy VK ex Lazy VK's Trinket Miclanjo (major pointed), was born in August 1984, bred by Carolyn Mooney and owned by John A. Mooney, Jr., Rockville, Maryland. She finished her championship at age 10 months with three majors. Pictured completing her title under Dr. Leon Seligman at Mountaineer Kennel Club taking Best of Winners and Best of Opposite Sex.

2. Ch. Pittore's Miz Minnie Mouse pictured winning a Group 2nd placement at Salisbury K.C. May 1978 under judge Wilma Hunter. Bred by Oz Kennels, co-owned by A. Mellinger and Pat Kirms.

3. Ch. Pittore's Harvest Dancer, National Specialty winner; Group winner; and Best of Variety at the A.K.C. Centennial Dog Show in November 1984. Patricia Pittore, owner, Goshen, Massachusetts.

4. Ch. Pittore's Lasting Little Hope earning a Group placement. Owned by Patricia Pittore, Goshen, Massachusetts.

5. Ch. Terrymont Marsubri Ragtime, Smooth Coat Chihuahua, Winner at the American Kennel Club Centennial Dog Show, November 1984, handled by Joyce McComiskey for co-breeders-owners Ruth H. Terry and Marcia Greenburg. The judge, Barbara Jarmoluk. Terrymont Kennels, Weston, Connecticut.

6. Ch. Gerbrock Double Dose Pittore winning Best in Sweepstakes at Longshore-Southport in 1985. Handled by Joyce McComiskey.

7. Ch. Pittore's Macho Man taking Best in Show, judged by the author, at Chihuahua Club of Atlanta Specialty in April 1980. Joyce McComiskey handled this outstanding little dog for breeder-owner Pat Pittore. One of the trophies which accompanied Macho Man's victory was a chic Mexican hat.

8. The well-known Group winner, Ch. Pittore's Harvest Dancer, taking Best of Breed at the Chihuahua Club of America National Specialty in May 1985. Joyce McComiskey handled, as usual, for Patricia Pittore, Goshen, Massachusetts.

1. Okatoma's On My Honor, by Herron's CR Sandman ex Lacey's Carmalitta, sitting on a ramp leading from the Chihuahua room window at Okatoma to a fenced yard. Breeder-owner, Patricia Lambert, Hattiesburg, Mississippi.

2. Litter sisters! Ch. Brite Star Queen of The Galaxy (Long Coat) and Ch. Brite Star Galactic Magic (Smooth Coat) are owned by Ms. Elizabeth Bickel, Kansas City, Missouri.

3. Ch. Thumbelina, who is Ch. Wee Tinker Belle's pup. Shown across Western Canada by her breeder-owner Donald Hunt, this 2½-3 pound charmer scored many exciting wins and Group placements. Owned by Heldon's Chihuahuas, Helen Hunt and Donald Hunt, Winnipeg, Manitoba, Canada.

4. Ch. RJR Reginald of Bayard, bred by RJR Chihuahuas, owned by Melanie Newell, Cambridge, Maryland. This little dog is the sire of 20 champions as of September 1985.

5. Kim at five months old, by Shinybrook Kokomo Kid ex Shinybrook Kinda, is typical of the Chihuahua puppies raised at Shinybrook Kennels.

6. Brite Star Orion, C.D., Dog World Award winner, in training for his C.D.X. performs the "broad jump" in super style. Ms. Elizabeth Bickel, owner, Kansas City, Missouri.

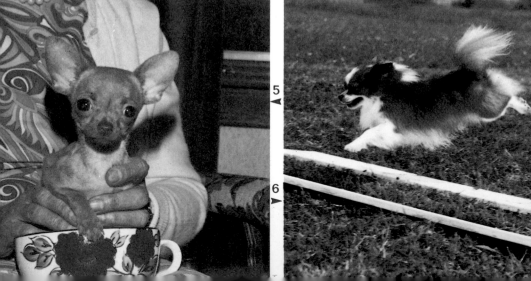

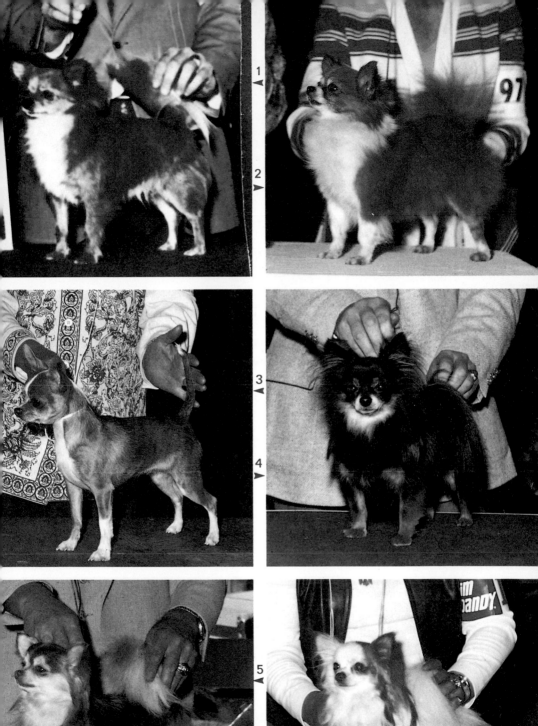

← Overleaf:

1. A proud moment in dog show history as the Long Coat Ch. Flint's Lil' Lucky Robin becomes the first and to date *only* Long Coat male Chihuahua in the United States to win an all-breed Best in Show, the occasion the Cincinnati Kennel Club Dog Show in May 1979, the judge Mrs. Thelma Brown. Jim Lehman handled for breeder Robert and Patsy Flint, Dayton, Ohio. Lucky Robin was sired by Ch. Shroyers Jeri Robin ex Flint's Happy Go Lucky Girl.

2. Ch. Komo's Tao Keno Reno winning Best Veteran at the Chihuahua Club of America, October 1984. Born July 1975, bred, owned and handled by Katherine J. Hood, Altamont, Illinois. He is the son of Komo's Tao Amo.

3. This blue-brindle Smooth is Ch. Pittore's Rainbow. Owner-handled by Patricia Pittore to a Best of Variety win.

4. Ch. Flint's Carbon Copy Robin taking Best of Variety at Westminster in 1983 for breeder-owners Robert L. and Patsy Sue Flint, Dayton, Ohio.

5. Ch. Miclanjo Wilhewag of Lazy VK, by Ch. Miclanjo Jimeniz Jones ex Lazy VK Koala Hermana Bear, born May 1983, was bred by Kathleen Brown and is owned and handled by John A. Mooney, Jr. At the age of 25 months, this Chihuahua has been Best of Variety on 31 occasions and has nine Group placements. Pictured winning Group 2nd at Kittanning Kennel Club in June 1985.

6. Ch. Lucky's Dickie Chip of Oz, the Mellingers' foundation sire and a Top Producer of seven champions, pictured at his first show in 1976 winning at Union County under judge Mrs. Ruth Turner. Dickie Chip was bred by Oz Kennels and Dick Dickerson.

1. Ch. Shinybrook Peter Panache, by Mex. and Am. Ch. Pittore's Peter Pan ex Shinybrook Miz Bug, taking Best of Winners at the A.K.C. Centennial Dog Show at Philadelphia, Pennsylvania, 1984. Owned by Shinybrook Kennels, Nancy Shonbeck, Westmoreland, New Hampshire.

2. Ch. Flint's Joy of Dandy Bandino, by Ch. Flint's Dandy Bandido ex Flint's Lil Pretty Priss, winning Best of Variety at Livonia in 1981 for owners Robert and Patsy Flint, Dayton, Ohio. Handled by Jim Lehman.

3. Ch. Quachitah's For Your Eyes Only, a multiple Best in Show winner, was Best in Toy Group at Westminster 1984, the first and only time a member of the breed has attained *this* victory. Bred and owned by Linda George, Waukesha, Wisconsin. Pictured winning the Best of Variety en route to Group 1st at Westminster.

4. Ch. Will O'Wisp Lil Boy Buttons taking Best of Variety at the Puyallup Valley Dog Fanciers in 1985. Bred, owned and handled by Millie F. Williams, Spokane, Washington. Buttons is by Ch. Lazy VK's Tomba Will O'Wisp ex Will O'Wisp Lil Stardust Sno.

5. Ch. Mignon's Amyis Micha, Best of Winners at Paducah in 1985, en route to the title. Owned by Mignon Murray, Mignon's Chihuahuas, Jacksonville, Florida.

6. Ch. Tiny Mite's Red Reagan, by Tiny Mite's Red Rambler ex Tiny Mite's Carmellow, taking points towards the title handled by Jim Lehman for Tiny Mite Chihuahuas, Robert L. DeJonge, Zeeland, Michigan.

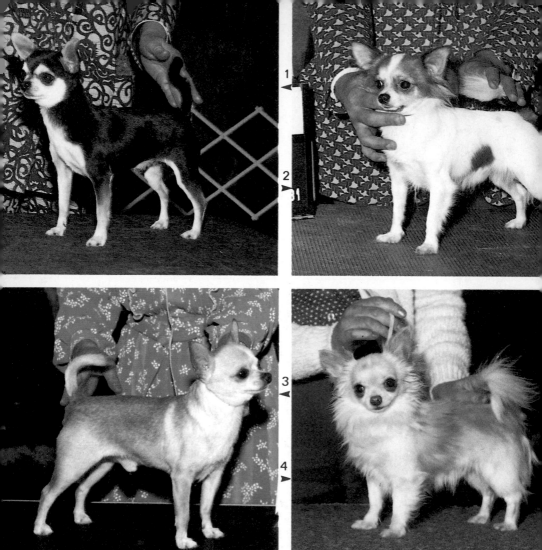

← **Overleaf:**

We love this portrait of the blue and tan Smooth Coat Chihuahua Eric's Misty Blue of Oz, by Ch. Don Joaquin Federico Chanel ex Lucky Coriand McFudget of Oz. Bred by Annette Mellinger, owned by Jo Ann Eagen. Has both majors to his credit.

1. Ch. Hack's Pack Golden Imp, by Ch. Duggar's Black Imp ex Shasta's Daisy, here is taking Winners en route to the title at Wine County K.C. in 1983 for owner Pat Porreca, Golden Bay Chihuahuas, Pleasanton, California.

2. The consistent Group winning Ch. Pittore's Harvest Dancer here is taking Best Toy at Western Reserve K.C. in 1984. Joyce McComiskey handled for Patricia Pittore, Goshen, Massachusetts.

3. Ch. Eric's Precious Munchkin Chip Oz, bred and owned by A. Mellinger and Eric Mellinger, Matawan, New Jersey, was sired by Ch. Lucky's Dickie Chip of Oz ex Eric's Hallelujah Dazzle of Oz. Pictured taking Best of Opposite Sex Long Coat at Hunterdon Hills in 1982. Handled by Mike Smith.

4. Ch. Bayard Tinkerbelle of Alvin, bred by Melanie Newell, owned by B. Paulouski, was Reserve Winners at the Michigan Specialty in 1982. Bred by Melanie Newell, Bayard Chihuahuas, Cambridge, Maryland.

5. At the Chihuahua Club of America National Specialty in 1981, Champion Call's Delightful Design, Smooth Coat, takes the Best of Breed award. Owner-handled by her breeder, Annie D. Call, Kaysville, Utah.

6. Ch. Elh's Mighty Lunar of Dartan, Best in Show winner owned by Golden Bay Chihuahuas, Pat and Bob Porreca, Pleasanton, California. By Ch. Handwerk's Lucky Strike ex Darton's Narona, this handsome and exciting little dog was bred by Darwin and Tanya Delaney. Pictured here winning the Toy Group at San Joaquin K.C., June 1985.

7. Ch. Hack Pack's Velvet Imp taking Best of Opposite Sex at Richmond Dog Fanciers in 1984 for owner Pat Porreca, Pleasanton, California.

8. Ch. Goldenbay's Moonglow of Hack's Pack, by Ch. Elh Mighty Lunar of Dartan, here taking Winners Bitch at Rogue Valley in 1984. Owned by Pat Porrecca, Pleasanton, California.

131

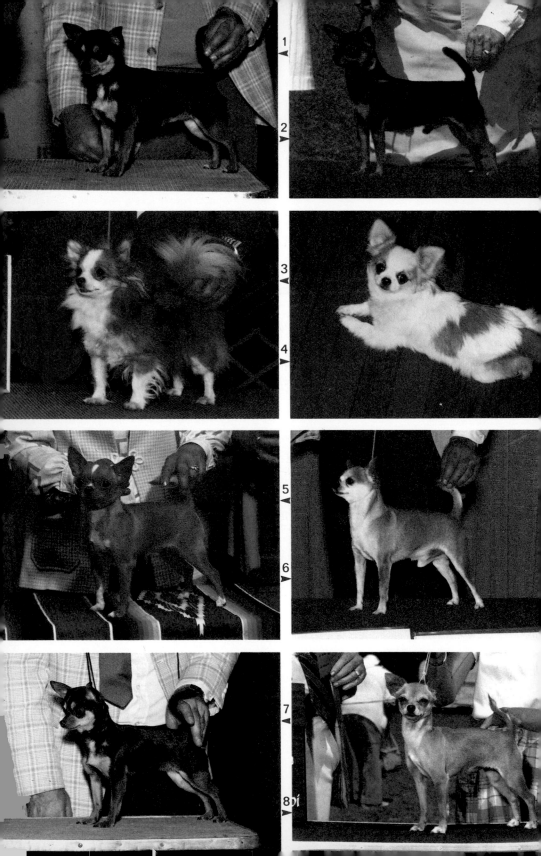

← **Overleaf:**

1. Ch. Okatoma Herron's I've Got Class surrounded by friends! This lovely bitch, by Herron's CR Sandman ex Lacey's Carmalita, was bred and owner handled to her championship by owner, Patricia Lambert, Okatoma Kennels, Hattiesburg, Mississippi.

2. Brite Star puppies "investigate" another type of Chihuahua. Ms. Elizabeth Bickel, Kansas City, Missouri.

3. A line-up of Brite Star Obedience Chihuahuas. *Left* to *right,* Tasir, C.D.X.; Ch. Queenie, Ch. Charlie, Orion, C.D.; Coco, C.D.X.; Apollo, C.D.; Ch. Chrissy, C.D.; and Daisy. All are working towards new obedience titles. Owned by Ms. Elizabeth Bickel, Kansas City, Missouri.

4. Ch. Call's Delightful Design awaiting her puppies. Owned by Chester P. and Annie D. Call, Kaysville, Utah.

5. Ch. Wee Tinker Belle was the foundation bitch for Don Hunt and Helen Hunt's Heldon Chihuahuas. A highly successful producer as well as show bitch.

6. Eladrew's Polly Flinders is a noted English winner with one Challenge Certificate towards her championship and many important wins to her credit. Owned by Eileen Lucas, Mansfield, Notts, England.

7. Chihuahua puppies enjoying a game. The Long Coat, Dolandi King Swinger, born May 22, 1982, by Ch. Dolandi Godolphinsson ex Dolandi Harmony Bell. The Smooth Coat, Dolandi Victor Ludorum, born November 1981, by Dolandi Oliver ex Dolandi Rise and Shine. Owned by Dolandi Chihuahuas, Diana and Laurence Fitt-Savage, owners, Sandringham, Norfolk, England.

8. Three enchanting Long Coat Chihuahua puppies by Ch. Tiny Mite's Terrific ex Tiny Mite's Opalina. These homebreds are owned by Robert L. DeJonge, Zeeland, Michigan.

Overleaf: →

1. Okatoma's Mr. Cool, C.D.X., by Jackie's Little Sugar Daddy ex Lacey's Wee Botique, bred and owned by Patricia Lambert, Hattiesburg, Mississippi.

2. This beautiful Smooth Chihuahua, Stephens Chip of Oz, was bred by A. Mellinger of Oz Chihuahuas and is owned by Mrs. Emma Stephens, well-known Toy judge and former breeder, Matawan, New Jersey.

3. A lovely study of JP's Pequena Dolly bred and owned by Judy Padgug, Sacramento, California.

4. Brace practice! Closest to front is JP's Pequena Dolly; behind her is mama, Ch. JP's Pequena Amiga. Judy Padgug, owner, JP Chihuahuas, Sacramento, California.

5. Ch. H and J's Blue Impy, dam of several nice champions, as a baby shows the coloring of a newborn blue Chihuahua. Jack and Hilda Phariss, owners, Bryan, Texas.

6. Tiny Mite's Moonbeam in 1974. Homebred by Robert L. DeJonge, Tiny Mite Chihuahuas, Zeeland, Michigan.

135

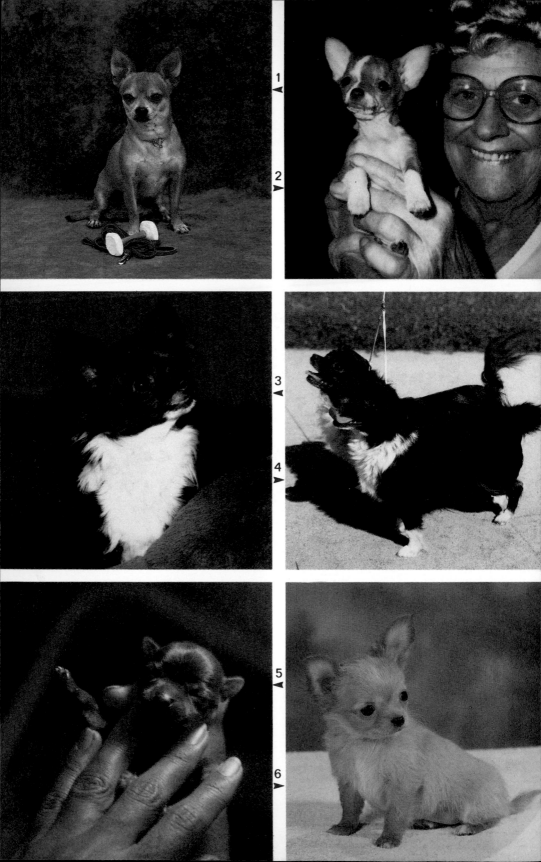

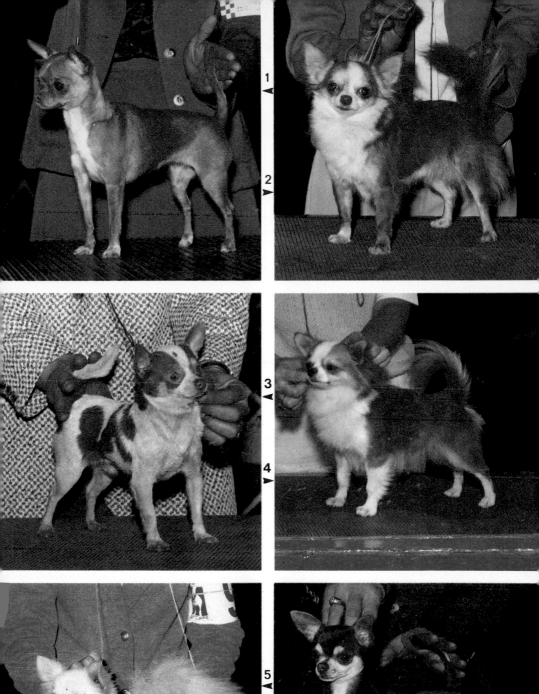

1 ◄

2 ◄

3 ◄

4 ◄

5 ◄

6 ◄

← **Overleaf:**

1. Ch. Heldon's Golden Honey Bee, an outstanding producer as well as highly successful in show competition. Don Hunt and Mrs. Helen Hunt, Heldon Chihuahuas, Winnipeg, Manitoba, Canada.

2. Ch. Komo's Tao Don Troubedor, born May 1980, handsome winning Long Coat with Group placements to his credit. Owned and handled by Katherine J. Hood, Altamont, Illinois.

3. Ch. Holiday's Spot Silver was sired by Varga's Silver David Tijuana ex Varga's Sweet Chocolate. Bred and owned by Mary Myers, Phoenix, Arizona, who sold her as a foundation bitch to Taiwan's only Chihuahua breeder.

4. Ch. H and J's Mystic Wizard, Best of Winners at the Chihuahua Club of America and Houston Chihuahua Club Specialties, pictured taking Best of Variety at Baytown Kennel Club, 1985, under judge Jane Forsyth. Marion Mondshine handled for owners Jack and Hilda Phariss, Bryan, Texas. A promising Long Coat special and already an excellent sire.

5. Ch. Komo's Tao Wagtime Cowboy Joe, born in July 1982, is a littermate to Ch. Komo's Tao Rootin' Tootin' Joye. Owned by Katherine Hood, Altamont, Illinois.

6. Ch. H and J's Perfecta Pan, litter sister to Ch. H and J's Peanut Pan. Handled here by Jim Lehman for owners, H and J Chihuahuas, Bryan, Texas.

1. Ch. Holiday's Tijuana La Cune was sired by Varga's Tijuana Midnite Snack ex Holiday's Hot Butterscotch. She is an all-breed Best in Show winner; a National Specialty winner; winner of 46 Group placements and 83 times Best of Variety; and the dam of two champions with another of promise. Bred and owned by Mary Myers, Holiday Chihuahuas, Phoenix, Arizona.

2. Ch. Heldon's El Campeador at Brandon handled by Sue Rempel for owners Donald Hunt and Mrs. Helen Hunt, Heldon Chihuahuas, Winnipeg, Manitoba, Canada. Here winning a Group placement under judge Anne Rogers Clark.

3. Ch. Holiday Tijuana Johnny, by Ch. Holiday's Hershey Bar ex Ch. Holiday's Tijuana La, a tiny two-and-a-half pound male, was bred by Mary Myers, Phoenix, Arizona, and is owned by Morris Lichtenstein, Corpus Christi, Texas. Taking Best of Winners here at Muncie K.C. handled by Jim Lehman.

4. Ch. Pittore's Walking Tall, the winner of five Group 1sts and 12 additional Group placements, here is winning one of them under judge Joe Faigel. Owned by Patricia Pittore and Cindy Balealb.

5. Ch. Holiday Earthquake McGoon, by Ch. Varga's Richardo De Oro ex Holiday Elvira, finished his title in January 1984. This sire of many outstanding puppies is owned and handled by breeder, Mary Myers, Holiday Chihuahuas, Phoenix, Arizona.

6. Aust. Ch. Elfredo Sir Galahad has amassed 458 Challenge Points at only four years of age. Owned by Mrs. Debbie Browne, Sydney, Australia.

7. Ch. Holiday Punchinella, by Holiday's Lil Ricky De Oro ex Holiday's Tijuana Tilly, is a homebred owned by Mary Myers, Phoenix, Arizona. This gorgeous dog is believed to be the only pure white Smooth Coat Chihuahua in the U.S., and is the sire of three white puppies. Mrs. Myers, who has been attempting to develop a white strain, now has three generations of them.

8. Donald Hunt winning a Group 1st with Ch. Tris-Tan's Peter Pan. Owned by Heldon Kennels, Helen and Donald Hunt, Winnipeg, Manitoba, Canada.

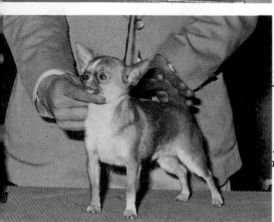

← Overleaf:

1. Ch. H and J's Peanuts Pan on her way to a Group 3rd. Handled by Walter Green. Peanut was Best Smooth Puppy at the Chihuahua Club of America Specialty in Baltimore in 1984. Owned by Jack and Hilda Phariss, Bryan, Texas.

2. Ch. Flint's Precious Jewel Robin winning Best of Variety for breeder-owners Robert L. and Patsy Sue Flint, Dayton, Ohio.

3. Ch. Brite Star Queen of the Galaxy is Best Puppy in Sweepstakes, Chihuahua Club of Oklahoma, Best Puppy in Show, Chihuahua Club of America week-end in Maryland; and Reserve Winners Bitch Chihuahua Club of America and Chihuahua Club of Maryland Specialties. Pictured taking Best of Opposite Sex, Chihuahua Club of Oklahoma, May 1984. This lovely Long Coat owned by Brite Star Chihuahuas, Ms. Elizabeth Bickel, Kansas City, Missouri.

4. Ch. Jo-El's Prince Charming owned by Mignon Murray, Jacksonville, Florida, taking Best of Winners to complete title at Thronateeska K.C. in February 1985.

5. Ch. Dartan Dominique D'Quachitah winning the Toy Group at Minneapolis in February 1982. An All-breed and Specialty Best in Show winner bred by Darwin and Tanya Delaney; owned by Linda George, Waukesha, Wisconsin.

6. Donald Hunt proudly handled his Ch. Sha-Na-Na to one of many Best of Variety wins. Owned by Heldon Chihuahuas, Don and Mrs. Helen Hunt, Winnipeg, Manitoba, Canada.

7. Ch. Flint's Lil Kandi Dancer Robin, by Ch. Flint's Lucky Jim Robin, taking Best of Opposite Sex to Best of Breed at the Detroit Specialty in 1980. Jim Lehman handled for Robert and Patsy Flint, Dayton, Ohio.

8. Long Coat Chihuahuas winning Best Brace in Show at Mississippi Valley K.C. in June 1982 under Judge Haworth Hoch. This brace owned and bred by Katherine J. Hood, Komo Chihuahuas, Altamont, Illinois.

1. Five generations of Brite Star Chihuahuas. *Left to right:* Brite Star Polaris of Shroyer, great granddam, age seven years; Brite Star Galactica, six-year-old granddam; Brite Star Andromeda, dam, age five years; Ch. Brite Star Little Dipper, 1½-year-old son; and Brite Star Aurora, 6-month-old granddaughter. Polaris is also Aurora's dam (Aurora's sire is Little Dipper) as well as her great-great grandmother. All owned by Ms. Elizabeth Bickel, Kansas City, Missouri.

2. A handsome trio of Tiny Mite Chihuahuas owned by Robert L. DeJonge, Zeeland, Michigan.

3. One of the first Long Coat litters at Tiny Mite's Kennels exemplifies the type for which fanciers are breeding. Robert L. DeJonge, Zeeland, Michigan.

1▲

2▲   3▲

← Overleaf:

1. A "clean sweep" for two exciting Chihuahua puppies! When only seven months old, JP's Pequena Dolly is awarded Best of Breed from the Bred-by-Exhibitor Class at Oakland Kennel Club in August 1984 as her litter brother, Macho, places Best of Opposite Sex, also from the classes. Both these awards gained over specials under Chihuahua authority judge Mrs. Wilma Hunter. Dolly is owned by Judy Padgug; Macho by Denise Grey and Virginia French. These two are by Ch. Stuber's Erik of Wildwood ex Ch. JP's Pequena Amiga. Bred by Judy Padgug.

2. "Tiny but tough" is an often used phrase in describing a Chihuahua. To fully understand its meaning, just look at this picture of Little Tinker Boy, aged two years at that time. Note the sturdiness of this little dog, who really seems not to consider himself tiny at all! Heldon Chihuahuas, Helen and the late Donald Hunt, owners, Winnipeg, Manitoba, Canada.

3. High In Trial winner, Ch. Brite Star Christmas Canis, owned by Brite Star Chihuahuas, Ms. Elizabeth Bickel, Kansas City, Missouri.

4. Winners Dog and Best of Variety, Smooth Coat, at Gallatin K.C. 1985. Ch. Will O'Wisp Lil Ruff N'Rowdi on the *left,* by Greenpoint Blackjack ex Will O'Wisp Lil Baby Snooks, bred, owned, and handled by Millie F. Williams, Spokane, Washington. On the *right,* Will O'Wisp Lil Spoka Lana.

1. America's #1 Chihuahua Obedience Brace. Brite Star Christmas Dream, C.D.X., on *left;* Glaisdaleast Fantasia, C.D.X. (foundation bitch at this kennel imported from England) on *right.* Ms. Elizabeth Bickel, Brite Star Chihuahuas, Kansas City, Missouri.

2. Debrajay Lady Avon and Debrajay Sir Lancellot are two homebred puppies by Aust. Ch. Elfreda Sir Galahad. Bred by Mrs. Debbie Browne, Sydney, Australia.

3. Ch. Pratt's Hal Festus Haggon, son of the Top Producing dog Ch. Hale's Bonansa Little Joe, is one of the handsome Chihuahuas from Pratt's Chihuahuas; Dorothy A. Pratt, Lakeland, Florida.

4. Two generations of Brite Star Obedience Titlists. Glaisdale East, on *left,* is the dam; Brite Star Apollo, C.D.X., on *right,* is the son. Owned by Ms. Elizabeth Bickel, Kansas City, Missouri.

5. Ch. Lakeview Leperchaun, foundation sire of Dorothy A. Pratt's well-known Pratt's Chihuahuas at Lakeland, Florida.

6. Dartan's Connie, Top Producing Chihuahua Dam, Top Producing Toy Dam with five champion offspring for 1984, and a total of nine champions as of mid-1985. By Ch. Dartan's Super Dude ex Dartan's Pitty Beth. Bred and owned by Darwin and Tanya Delaney, Essexville, Michigan.

1 ▶
2 ▶
3 ▶
4 ▶
5 ▶
6 ▶

← Overleaf:

1. Ch. Mignon's Dixie, a lovely Long Coat, is described by owner Mignon Murray, Mignon's Chihuahuas, Jacksonville, Florida, as her "Champion Companion."

2. Okatoma's Blaze Away Gremlin, by Ch. Ellen's Little Blaze Bandito ex Wee Windsom Windy, at three months won a Group 4th at eight months under Mrs. V.M. Olivier. Bred by Pat Rose and Jean Norton. Owned by Patricia Lambert, Okatoma Chihuahuas, Hattiesburg, Mississippi. A truly outstanding Chihuahua puppy!

3. Ch. H and J's Perfecta Pan as a puppy enjoying the sunshine. Jack and Hilda Phariss, Bryan, Texas.

4. JP's Pequena Dolly bait training for the ring. The ideal way to make your dog "look alert" during judging is the use of a small bit of liver or some other well-loved delicacy to keep him at attention. Dolly belongs to Judy Padgug, Sacramento, California.

5. Ch. Okatoma's Lickidy Split, by Mi Vida's Lucky Star, C.D. ex Pete's Whiskey Lady, C.D. Bred, owned and handled by Patricia Lambert, Okatoma Chihuahuas, Hattiesburg, Mississippi. A champion from the puppy classes, "Skeeter" is now starting on her obedience career, carrying on in the family tradition.

6. Dolandi King Swinger among the hyacinths. Born January 1982 by English Ch. Dolandi Godolphinsson ex Dolandi Harmony Bell, was three months old in this picture taken April 1982. Now a consistent winner at the championship shows. Owned by Dolandi Chihuahuas, Diana and Laurence Fitt-Savage, Sandringham, Norfolk, England.

1. Ch. Dartan's Constant Comment, by Ch. Dartan's Pirate Blackbeard ex Dartan's Connie, here is winning Best of Opposite Sex at the Chihuahua Club of America Specialty Show in 1985. She has 19 Group placements as of mid-1985. Bred and owned by Darwin and Tanya Delaney, for whom Linda George handled under judge Maxine Beam.

2. Shinybrook Charisma Captain, by Lucky's Love Button of Oz ex Shinybrook Charisma Mina, taking Winners Dog in Long Coats at the Chihuahua Club of America Specialty in May 1985. Owned by Shinybrook Chihuahuas, Westmoreland, New Hampshire.

3. Ch. Pratt's Oliver Blue, blue and tan Smooth Coat finished in 1985. Owned by Dorothy A. Pratt, Lakeland, Florida.

4. Ch. Okatoma's Little Bita Whiskey, by Herron's CR Sandman ex Pete's Whiskey Lady C.D. bred by Rae Lambert, owned and handled by Patricia Lambert, Hattiesburg, Mississippi. Bita finished in nine shows going Best of Breed over specials for her first two majors. She has a Group 2nd and a Group 4th all prior to her 9-month birthday.

5. Ch. Shinybrook's Gingersnap started out owned by Mrs. Shonbeck, then went to California to Jeff Nokes.

6. Ch. Heldon's Princess Naomi has seven Group 1sts; five seconds; and some thirds and fourths to her credit. Here winning Best Toy at Portage K.C. in June 1985. By Can. and Am. Ch. Hilaire's Cher Soleil ex Ch. Sha-Na-Na, she was bred by Mrs. Helen Hunt, Heldons Chihuahuas, Winnipeg, Manitoba, Canada.

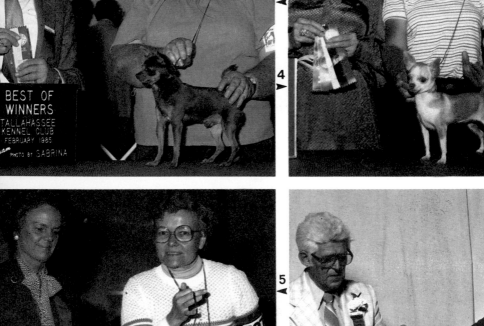

BEST OF
WINNERS

TALLAHASSEE
KENNEL CLUB
FEBRUARY 1985

PHOTO BY SABRINA

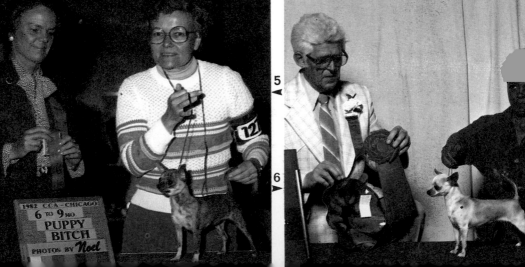

1982 CCA-CHICAGO
6 TO 9 MO
PUPPY
BITCH
PHOTOS BY Noel

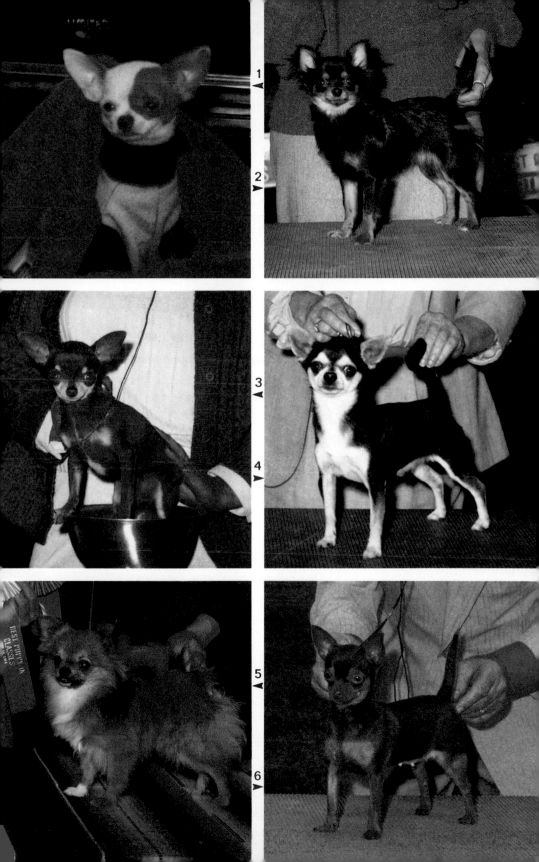

← Overleaf:

1. A Tiny Mite Chihuahua all bundled up against the cold. Owned by Robert L. De-Jonge, Zeeland, Michigan.

2. Lucky Eric's Electra of Oz, by Ch. Lucky's Woody Junior of Oz ex Lucky's Prunella of Oysart, was bred by Annette Mellinger and H. Wm. Ohman. Here taking Best of Variety at Naugatuck K.C. in 1985. Owned by Ginette E. Perez.

3. Winning a Toy Group in August 1979, Ch. Pittore's Lasting Little Hope. Handled by Joyce McComiskey for Patricia Pittore, Goshen, Massachusetts.

4. Joyce McComiskey handling Ch. Shinybrook Peter Panache to points towards the title under judge Dr. Leon Seligman at Tidewater Kennel Club in 1984. Nancy Shonbeck, owner.

5. Ch. Brite Star Little Dipper taking Best of Winners and Best Puppy at the Chihuahua Club of Oklahoma Specialty. Won two more majors from puppy class at the next two shows. Ms. Elizabeth Bickel, owner, Brite Star Chihuahuas, Kansas City, Missouri.

6. Can. and Am. Ch. Bridges Ardita Del Shillmaine, was a confirmed Canadian Champion in 1979 while still a puppy, finishing in U.S. during 1982. Has Group placements in the United States; and more than 80 such awards in Canada. Canada's #3 Chihuahua in 1982, #2 in 1984. Owned by Capt. A.M.W. Samuels, Shillmaine Chihuahuas, Mimico, Ontario, Canada.

1. Ch. Bayard Alvin of Reginald RJR is a homebred owned by Melanie Newell, Bayard Chihuahuas, Cambridge, Maryland. This handsome Long Coat is the sire of eight champions to date.

2. Three homebreds from Melanie Newell's kennels. They are, *left* to *right,* Bayard Belle, Blast, and Elf.

3. Sometimes puppies like to do a bit of teething on the furniture. All of which is forgiven when they grow up to become winners, as did Ch. Bayard Raw Silk of Reginald, bred and owned by Melanie Newell, Cambridge, Maryland.

4. How is this for adorable??? "Tinker" is owned and was bred by Tiny Mite Chihuahuas, Robert L. DeJonge, Zeeland, Michigan. Note how beautifully this obviously young puppy is already striking a show pose!

5. A beautiful portrait of Tiny Mite's Chocolate Taffy owned by Robert L. DeJonge, Zeeland, Michigan.

6. Young homebreds from Bayard Chihuahuas owned by Melanie Newell, Cambridge, Maryland.

1 ▶

2 ▶

3 ▶

4 ▶

5 ▶

6 ▶

1

2

3

4

5

6

← Overleaf:

1. Long Coat puppies by Ch. Tiny Mite's El Pepita ex Tiny Mite's Blondie Bea. Bred and owned by Robert L. DeJonge, Zeeland, Michigan. An interesting color study of young Chi puppies.

2. H and J's Cocoa Princess, Winners Bitch at the Dallas Chihuahua Club Specialty and a most cherished pet enjoys a vacation in Big Bend National Park with the state of Chihuahua in the far distance. H and J Kennels, Bryan, Texas.

3. Okatoma's Mr. Cool, C.D.X., "Fonzie," proudly carrying his dumb-bell. Patricia Lambert, owner, Hattiesburg, Mississippi.

4. Ch. Okatoma Herron's I've Got Class relaxing at home. Owned, bred, and handled to her title by Patricia Lambert, Okatoma Chihuahuas, Hattiesburg, Mississippi.

5. Merry Christmas for Ch. Okatoma's Lickedy Split, "Skeeter" to friends. Bred, owned, and handled by Patricia Lambert, Hattiesburg, Mississippi.

6. This handsome Long Coat is Ch. Eric's Benji Chip of Oz, by Ch. Lucky's Dickie Chip of Oz ex Eric's Hallayyah Dazzle of Oz. Bred and owned by Eric and Annette Mellinger, Oz, Matawan, New Jersey.

Overleaf: ⟶

1. Komo's Long Coat winners at Daytona, January 1982, under judge Joe Gregory. *Left to right,* Ch. Komo's Tao Don Troubedor, Best of Variety, in the arms of breeder-owner-handler Katherine Hood; Mr. Gregory; Ch. Joel's Gunner Chiloop of Komo, Winners Dog, owned by Katherine Hood and R. and J. Kruetzman; and Winners Bitch, Ch. Komo's Skylark Serenade, owner-handler Mrs. Lloyd Reeves, Georgetown, Florida.

2. Ch. Mignon's Queenie Duvall, handsome Smooth Chihuahua owned by Mignon Murray, Jacksonville, Florida.

1 ▲ 2 ▲

Chapter 7

Chihuahuas in Australia

As is the case wherever the breed is known, Chihuahuas are popular and well liked in Australia. They have attracted a group of knowledgeable breeders working with outstanding imported and Australian bloodlines from which lines of their own are being and have been created.

We are pleased to be in receipt of a letter from the Hon. Secretary of the Chihuahua Club of New South Wales, Mrs. Marcia Jackson, who issues a most cordial invitation to anyone interested in this club or its programs and activities to contact her. The New South Wales area is especially abundant in Chihuahua owners and there are some very true-to-type and high quality Chihuahuas to be found there.

Mrs. Jackson enclosed with her note one of the car stickers which feature the club emblem; also a truly lovely membership pin which is beautifully done with examples of the two Varieties of Chihuahua depicted in head study, highlighted by blue enamel background for the lettering. A very attractive piece of jewelry for Chihuahua fans.

On the following pages we bring you some kennel stories from Australia. We feel sure that our readers will find them interesting, and that the type and quality of the Chihuahuas there will be sincerely admired. Many of the current Chihuahuas in Australia trace

Two handsome Chihuahuas from "down under." They are, (*left*) Aust. Ch. Al-haja Joshua, four-pound red Smooth dog, born in 1981; and (*right*) Aust. Ch. Alhaja Eclaire, chocolate and tan Smooth bitch, born in 1982, weight three and a half pounds. They are owned by Alhaja Kennels, Mike and Diana Stone, Duffy's Forest, New South Wales.

their ancestry back to Mrs. Thelma Gray and her Rozavels, which actually started in England, then came to Australia in later years where Mrs. Gray relocated and stayed for the remainder of her lifetime. Her dogs brought with them leading English bloodlines and, in the background, some dogs which she imported to England from the United States in the early days of her Chihuahua interest.

ALHAJA

Alhaja Chihuahuas, located in Duffy's Forest, New South Wales, belong to Mike and Diana Stone who have been dedicated breeders and exhibitors since the early 1970s. In fact, in order to pursue their hobby they moved from an exclusive suburb to five acres of land in the bush where they have established their kennel with a lot of heartbreak and a great deal of success.

The Stones have between 50 and 70 Chihuahuas, both coats, and although they built their kennels with every comfort, including wall heaters for their very mild winters, a great many sneak into the house at any given opportunity, making the family room well filled with baskets and with puppies. There is also a retirement village for the old bitches who have served them so well, where they can live out their lives in comfort, with good food and warm beds.

Besides being a superb show dog, the Stones' Australian Champion Alhaja Joshua has proven an outstanding sire. His daughter, Australian Champion Alhaja Eclaire, is one of the top winning bitches in New South Wales with many, many awards in her distinguished career. She was the Chihuahua Club of New South Wales Puppy of the Year in 1983 and again in 1984, although during the latter year she was eligible for only a very short period of time and won by gaining four Best of Breed awards in four shows. She then went on to become the Chihuahua Club of New South Wales Dog of the Year for 1984.

There is also another Joshua daughter in the ring doing exceptionally well, plus a Minor daughter just taking off. Joshua's pedigree goes back to the Seggieden line in England, and while Eclaire's is the same through Josh being her sire, she picks up the American line of Thurmers through her maternal grandfather.

Joshua's show record includes the winning of his first Challenge Certificate as a Minor at the age of seven months. During the fol-

Aust. Ch. Chilula Sable Laddie owned by B. Madden is representative of the splendid Chihuahuas at Australia's Chilula Kennels.

lowing years he has had numerous awards including In Show and several Toy Groups. The highlight of Joshua's career was his great win at the Royal Easter Show, Sydney, in 1984 under the Mexican judge Senor R. F. Hernandez when he took Challenge Dog from an outstanding line-up and was then awarded Best of Breed by the same judge. Three days later, at the prestigious Chihuahua Club of New South Wales Specialty, Josh again took out Best of Breed under Mrs. June Weston of Canberra, A.C.T.

Joshua was out of one of the first litters from cross mating long with smooth coat after a five year trial period was granted the Australian breeders by the Kennel Control in New South Wales. His mother was a top winning bitch, black Long Coat Australian Champion Lanvilla Jenez, while his sire, a Smooth Coat, was Australian Champion Tadea Hannibal, also winner of numerous awards. Joshua was the Chihuahua Club of New South Wales Puppy of the Year in 1982.

Puppy of the Year and Dog of the Year trophies, for those of you who are unfamiliar with the Australian customs, are for point scores run over 15 and 10 top shows respectively over the year in which the dog or bitch was first required to win his/her class, and then Best Opposite, in order to become eligible for points. Eclaire followed in father Joshua's pawprints in October 1984 when she took out Best of Breed and Best in Show at the Chihuahua Club of New South Wales October Show in 1984 (the club holds two shows annually) under Miss V. Howe of Queensland.

Although Chihuahuas are the Stones' first love, they also breed Italian Greyhounds, having imported a bitch from England. She easily gained her Australian title and has recently whelped a litter by an American Champion, which is very exciting to this enthusiastic couple.

A car sticker from the Chihuahua Club of New South Wales, a very busy and energetic group of fanciers from Australia who work hard to protect the best interests of their breed in that area.

BROOK SHARN

Brook Sharn Chihuahuas at Harbord, New South Wales, are owned by Mr. and Mrs. H. M. Callaghan who are great enthusiasts of this breed. The Callaghans concentrate on the Long Coat Variety and have done so with considerable success.

Their Australian Champion BrookSharn Blue Starr has won most of the major shows in New South Wales. His most pleasing achievement has been the award of "Dog of the Year" for three years consecutively.

Australian Ch. BrookSharn Blue Starr, owned by Mr. H.M. Callaghan, Brook Sharn Chihuahuas, Harbord, New South Wales, is a sable Long Coat male who was born in 1981. Here he is pictured winning Best in Show at the Chihuahua Club of New South Wales Specialty in 1984. A handsome little dog with many accomplishments of which to be proud.

An informal snapshot of the lovely and noted Aust. Ch. BrookSharn Blue Starr, a sire of champions as well as an important winner. Owned by Mr. H.M. Callaghan.

Blue Starr's litter sister, Australian Champion BrookSharn Royal Butterfly has also done well at the shows.

Two out of three of Blue Starr's daughters have gained their Australian Championships, including Champion Chilula Calypso Girl.

Blue Starr and Royal Butterfly are by Australian Champion Keitoy Royal Starr ex Chilulu Blue Butterfly. Royal Starr is by Morrilyn Christopher (son of Australian Champion Morrilyn St. Nicholas) while Blue Butterfly traces back to St. Nicholas and to several of the Rozavel champions.

Mrs. Callaghan also noted another "family member," Australian Champion Chilula Sable Laddie, who is owned by B. Madden and is a great-uncle to Blue Starr.

CHICHENITZA

Chichenitza Chihuahuas are at Concord in New South Wales

where they are owned by Mrs. Marcia Jackson.

Pride of this kennel is the lovely and highly successful Smooth Coat male, Australian Champion Chichenitza Inca Gold who was born in August 1979 and who is a homebred. Sired by Chinchorro Gepetto ex Chichenitza Roselle, Inca Gold traces back in his pedigree to such famous names as Australian Champion Tampico Wee Robbie and Australian Champion Jodoca Brando Cheree (the latter by Australian Champion Tampico Poco Sandy ex Australian Champion Soltilo Gidget Mia), Australian Champion Salinacruz Miss Muffet, and the English Champions Kingsmere Merry Mascot (U.K. import) and Rozavel Large As Life.

In the show ring, Inca Gold's career has been distinguished. He won Challenge Dog at the Sydney Royal Easter Show in both 1981 and 1982. He was winner of the Chihuahua Club's Puppy of the Year Trophy in 1981. He was Best of Breed and Best State Bred at the October 1981 Chihuahua Club Championship Show.

Inca Gold acquired his title of Australian Champion at the Sydney Royal held on April 18, 1981.

Aust. Ch. Chichenitza Inca Gold owned by Mrs. Marcia Jackson, Chichenitza Chihuahuas, Concord, New South Wales.

Aust. Ch. Elfreda Sir Galahad, famous Australian winner, owned by Mrs. Debbie Browne, Sydney.

DEBRAJAY

Debrajay Chihuahuas are owned by Mrs. Debbie Browne at Sydney. This is the home of the very famous Australian Champion Elfreda Sir Galahad, son of Elfreda Marco Polo ex Elfreda Lady Edwina. His breeder was Mrs. P. Burgess.

Sir Galahad, at only four years old, has a very exciting show career which has earned for him a total of 458 Challenge Points. His wins include Best of Breed at the 1984 Sydney Royal Easter Show; Runner Up to Best in Show, The Chihuahua Club of New South

Aust. Ch. Chilula Sable Laddie owned by B. Madden, New South Wales. Pictured with his award for Best State Bred in Show at the Chihuahua Club of New South Wales Specialty Show in 1981 where he was also awarded Champion Dog.

Wales; Best Minor Puppy in Show, The Chihuahua Club of New South Wales; Best Minor Puppy in Show, The New South Wales Womens Dog Club; Best Australian-bred in Show, Luddenham A H and I Society; Best Toy Exhibit, Sutherland A H and I Society; Runner-Up Best in Toy Group, Parramatta A B K C; Best Minor Puppy in Toy Group, Fairfield A B K C; Best Intermediate Toy Group, Wollongong A B K C; and Best Open in Toy Group, Liverpool A B K C.

Mrs. Browne has two lovely puppies coming along by Sir Galahad whom she hopes will make their presence felt in the ring as they mature. They are Debrajay Lady Avon and Debrajay Sir Lancellott. Their dam is Elfreda Gold Lily.

Chapter 8

The Standard of the Breed

The "standard of the breed" to which one hears and sees such frequent reference whenever purebred dogs are written of or discussed, is the word picture of what is considered to be the ideal specimen of the breed in question. It outlines, in minute detail, each and every feature of that breed, both in physical characteristics and in temperament, accurately describing the dog from whisker to tail, creating a clear impression of what is to be considered correct or incorrect, the features comprising "breed type," and the probable temperament and behavior patterns of typical members of that breed.

The standard is the guide for breeders endeavoring to produce quality Chihuahuas, and for fanciers wishing to learn what is considered beautiful in these dogs, and it is the tool with which judges evaluate the dogs in order to make their decisions in the show ring. The dog it describes is the one which we seek and to which we compare in making our evaluations. It is the result of endless hours spent in dedicated work by knowledgeable members of each breed's current Specialty Club (the Chihuahua Club of America, in this case), resulting from the combined efforts of the Club itself, its individual members, and finally the American Kennel Club by whom official approval must be granted prior to each standard's acceptance, or that of any amendments or changes to

Ch. Jo-El's Livin' Doll, by Ch. Dartan's Pirate Blackbeard ex Vanderpool's Tub of Love, a homebred from Jo-El Kennels, Joan and Russ Kruetzman, Creve Coeur, Missouri.

it, in the United States. Breed standards are based on intensive study of breed history in the United States and in the countries where these dogs originated or were recognized prior to introduction into the United States, and the purposes for which the breed was originally created and developed. All such factors have played a part in the drawing up of our present standards.

Ch. Glindale's Mighty Munchkin showing off the quality that has made him a famous winner. Owned by Linda M. Glenn, Harrington Park, New Jersey.

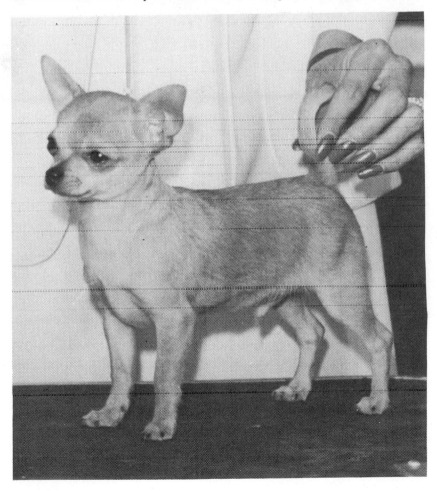

A moment of victory for a very young future star! This exquisite puppy bitch grew up to become Ch. Call's Delightful Desire. This was, I believe, her first dog show. Here she is winning Best in Sweepstakes from the Junior Puppy Class. Later that day she took Reserve Winners Bitch, again from junior puppies, under the author, the occasion having been the Chihuahua Club of Atlanta Specialty in April 1980.

OFFICIAL STANDARD FOR THE CHIHUAHUA IN THE UNITED STATES

HEAD: A well rounded "apple dome" skull with or without molera. Cheeks and jaws lean. Nose moderately short, slightly pointed (self-colored in blond types, or black). In moles, blues, and chocolates they are self-colored. In blond types, pink nose permissible.

EARS: Large, held erect when alert but flaring at the sides at about an angle of 45 degrees when in repose. This gives breadth between the ears. In *Long Coats*, ears fringed. (Heavily fringed ears may be tipped slightly, never down).

EYES: Full but not protruding, balanced, set well apart—dark ruby or luminous. (Light eyes in blond types permissible).

TEETH: Level or scissors bite. Overshot or undershot bite or any distortion of the bite should be penalized as a serious fault.

NECK AND SHOULDER: Slightly arched, gracefully sloping into lean shoulders, may be smooth in the very short types, or with ruff about neck preferred. In *Long Coats*, large ruff on neck desired and preferred. Shoulders lean, sloping into a slightly broadening support above straight forelegs that are set well under, giving a free play at the elbows. Shoulders should be well up, giving balance and soundness, sloping into a level back. (Never down or low). This gives a chestiness and strength of forequarters yet not of the "Bulldog" chest; plenty of brisket.

BACK AND BODY: Level back, slightly longer than height. Shorter backs desired in males. Ribs rounded (but not too much "barrel shaped").

HINDQUARTERS: Muscular with hocks well apart, neither out nor in, well let down with firm, sturdy action.

TAIL: Moderately long, carried sickle either up or out, or in a loop over the back with tip just touching the back. (Never tucked under). Hair on tail in harmony with the coat of the body, preferred furry in *Smooth Coats*. In *Long Coats*, tail full and long (as a plume).

FEET: Small, with toes well split up but not spread, pads cushioned, with fine pasterns. (Neither the hare nor the cat-foot.) A dainty, small foot with nails moderately long.

COAT: In the *Smooth* the coat should be soft texture, close and glossy. (Heavier coats with undercoats permissible). Coat placed well over back with ruff on neck and more scanty on head and ears. In *Long Coats* the coat should be of a soft texture, either flat or slightly curly with undercoat preferred. Ears fringed (heavily fringed ears may be tipped slightly, never down), feathering on feet and legs, and pants on hind legs. Large ruff on neck desired and preferred. Tail full and long (as a plume).

COLOR: Any color—solid, marked or splashed.

WEIGHT: A well balanced little dog not to exceed six pounds.

GENERAL APPEARANCE: A graceful, alert, swift-moving little dog with saucy expression. Compact, and with terrier-like qualities.

SCALE OF POINTS

Head, including Ears 20
Body, including Tail 20
Coat...20
Legs 20
General Appearance and Action...20
Total 100

DISQUALIFICATIONS
Cropped tail, bobtail.
Broken down or cropped ears.
Any dog over 6 pounds in weight.
In Long Coats, too thin coat that resembles bareness.

Approved November 14, 1972

INTERPRETATION OF THE STANDARD

Learning the words of a standard is not the least bit difficult. Many people are able to recite verbatim the one for their "very own" breed (and sometimes others, too, if theirs is a retentive memory). The trick is to learn to *interpret* that standard; to truly understand what the words are saying; and to do so thoroughly enough as to enable you to close your eyes and see a mental picture of the very dog that standard is describing as ideal. *That* is the knowledge which will make you truly *understanding* of your breed. And it is a "must" if one is to acquire the ability to evaluate, compare, and make decisions between several individuals; or choose a good one as opposed to one which is lacking in type.

What sort of Chihuahua do *you* picture as you read the standard? It should be a most important looking little dog; small and dainty but at the same time impressive by its "dogginess," its alert "here I am" attitude; its well coordinated balance; and its proud, gay carriage. A Chihuahua should *never* be a cringing, timid looking dog; rather, it should remind one of a small Terrier, alert, inquisitive, ready for anything.

One's first impression upon studying a Chihuahua should be that it is well balanced; i.e., skull and foreface in correct proportion to one another, the head in correct proportion to the neck and body, legs of proper length and bone. The Chihuahua is a breed whose back is slightly longer than the height of the dog at the withers; thus a low-slung, short legged look is undesirable and atypical.

Breed type in a Chihuahua is largely distinguished by the correct head and ears. Bear in mind that the ears are to be large and flaring at the sides when the dog is relaxed, *not* narrow and carried stiffly erect, the latter desired only when the dog is at attention. The skull is dome-shaped and nicely rounded, never flat on top, with good breadth between the ears. These ears, and the correct eyes, which must be full and wideset as opposed to narrow and slitlike, give the Chihuahua head its unique expression. The correct Chihuahua muzzle is considerably shorter than the skull (perhaps one third the length of the total head) and should be slightly pointed, cheeks and jaws clean. Without the correct head qualities the Chihuahua does not *look* like a Chihuahua, as much of the breed's unique individuality is to be seen right there.

Strangely, the two most damaging head faults—ears set too narrowly and carried bolt upright, and small slanting eyes—seem to go together. Why I cannot say; but you will notice, if you watch, that this truly is the case.

Another special breed characteristic of Chihuahuas is the "chesty" look, brought about by nicely rounded ribs and proper shoulder angulation. The brisket should be somewhat broader than too narrow, and the Chihuahua's air of importance is enhanced by his standing well up on his forefeet with strong, straight, well set forelegs. Remember that the Chihuahua foot is another distinction; it should be small with toes well split up, not tight and round like the foot of a cat, nor long and narrow like that of a hare. This does not mean that the foot should be flat and spread out—simply that the toes are separated. Pads should be well cushioned. And this is the only breed I can think of off-hand in which the nails are preferably moderately long.

A Chihuahua with proper front assemblage never "dips" nor "hollows out" at the withers. The topline should be level from withers to tail, and we are pleased to note during the past few years that breeders are achieving considerable improvement in this area although there is still a bit of work to be done.

Hindquarters are another important part of a correctly assembled Chihuahua. They should be broad at the hips, muscular, and firm, with good bend of stifle and hock joint, the hock straight and firm from joint to the paw. Thus the Chihuahua has good driving power from these hindquarters which flex nicely, keeping up with the correct reach of well assembled forequarters.

Since the coat of a Long Coat Chihuahua is what distinguishes this variety from the Smooth, it should be abundant, soft in texture, with proper undercoat; it should not be sparse and skimpy! Fringes should be profuse with a luxuriant plume and heavy fringing on the ears. A correctly coated Long Coat Chihuahua is elegant and beautiful, and the lack of coat in this variety does set one back considerably in gaining admiration and approval.

The so-called "Smooth" Chihuahua should also be well coated with thick, close, glossy hair. Many of these also have undercoat, which is allowed. And a ruff on the neck is desirable, so it should *not* be trimmed or thinned out.

The overall look of a Chihuahua should be one of compactness. The males are preferably shorter in body than the females (but the latter should *not* be long—only slightly more so than tall).

Remember that several Chihuahua colors have noses of that same color; and that while blond types may have black noses, in the blonds pink noses are also permissible and not to be penalized.

BRITISH VS. U.S. CHIHUAHUAS

The principal difference between the British and the United States Standards for Chihuahuas centers around disqualifications and around the points rating which are included in the U.S. but not in Britain.

The British list "faults to be penalized in accordance with their severity" rather than disqualifying for any condition other than demanding that male Chihuahuas be equipped with two normal testicles fully descended in the scrotum, which is a requirement also in America but stated in the A.K.C. rules rather than in the breed Standard.

One other difference has to do with the presence of molera, which is permitted in the U.S. but not mentioned in the British Standard. A molera being a condition described as an "incomplete or abnormal ossification of the skull."

Who could possibly resist so appealing a little dog as the Long Coat, English and American Ch. Apoco Deodar Best Suit, with whom Peter Green has won numerous outstanding honors following his brilliant career, which included 22 C.Cs., in Great Britain? "Sooty" belongs to Mary M. Silkworth, Jackson, Michigan.

Chapter 9

On Owning a Chihuahua

One can best appreciate the diversity of the Chihuahua's talents and personality when one stops to consider the very wide range of people who are devoted to this breed, would have no other, and can go on for hours about their charm and character. These people, surprisingly on first thought, range from the burliest, most "he-man" types to the petite and feminine ladies. Why is this true? It can only be due to the fact that the Chihuahua, although the smallest of all breeds, is firmly endowed with all the charm, intelligence, courage, and true "dogginess" of even the most giant of his canine "cousins." The only thing lacking in the Chihuahua is pure size and physical strength, which in many situations and cases makes him more desirable than a dog many times his size. Certainly he is not lacking in personality, nor vitality, nor in being full of fun and mischief. He combines big dog spirit in a small dog package; "tiny but tough" is a description that fits him well, and which explains why men as well as women and children consider him to be a very special dog.

Without doubt, the Chihuahua is one of the easiest, most convenient dogs to own. Just consider the assets of this diminutive size if you live in a small apartment (or even in a large one) in the city. How easy it is to just pick him up in elevators or stores, or many places where large dogs are unwelcome! His smallness makes a little exercise go a long way, so that if you are on a busy schedule, or one who does not enjoy long walks in the great outdoors, you need not feel obligated to force yourself for the sake of his health or well being. Actually a Chihuahua can get plenty of exercise having the free run of your house or apartment and can be trained to use a newspaper in lieu of outside facilities if you prefer to train him or her that way. This is a great convenience to folks in business or on schedules which sometimes necessitate long absences from home, as you know that he has his paper to use if necessary should you be delayed in returning.

As a pet owner, perhaps you hate boarding your dog when you go away. Again the Chihuahua's convenient size stands you in good stead. How easy it is to transport him in a small, lightweight (even with the dog inside) carrier! One which on planes can slip neatly beneath your seat! One can go visiting places with a little dog where a big dog would be greeted with horror! And even the most anti-dog motels and hotels could hardly object to six pounds of appeal arriving in his tiny carrier—or even trotting across the lobby on lead as though he owns the world.

The Chihuahua is probably one of the easiest breeds of all to care for on a daily basis. They require only a minimum of grooming, whether a Smooth or a Long Coat, as even the latter does not require the endless attention of many other coated breeds. A brushing every few days will keep either variety at its best with a bit of added attention to careful combing of the fringes and guarding against possible matting around the underneath (armpits, etc.) areas of the Longs. Frequent bathing is not necessary as these little dogs ordinarily stay clean and fresh with regular brushing. And think how little territory must be covered on a Chihuahua as compared to a medium sized or big dog!

About the only special protection needed by Chihuahuas is against cold and drafts. A Chihuahua going outdoors from a warm house or apartment should wear a sweater when the weather is cold (or even extra chilly) and a rain coat when it is stormy with either rain or snow. Feet, legs, and underneath should be dried when the dog returns indoors. And a warm bed free of drafts should be provided.

While perhaps you may not have thought about it that way, Chihuahuas make very good burglar alarm systems. True, they are

Pistol Pete of Lux, by Mitchell Max Rock Hill ex Mitchell Spot, in his truck. Bred by Roy Mitchell. Owned by Patricia Lambert, Okatoma Chihuahuas, Hattiesburg, Mississippi.

The Queen! Grindale's Lil Bit of Sampsen at home in her brass bed. Linda M. Glenn, owner, Glinwood Chihuahuas, Harrington Park, New Jersey.

Okatoma's Mr. Cool, C.D.X., "Fonzie" (*left*); Pete's Whiskey Lady, C.D. (*right*).
Two obedience "stars" owned by Patricia Lambert, Hattiesburg, Mississippi.

not of a size to intimidate a prowler by fear of attack. But they can work up a very big bit of agitation when a stranger or strange sound is noticed, causing an attention-drawing situation which is exactly what someone up to mischief is most anxious to avoid. Also, remember, a tiny dog darting about is very difficult to catch, thus not likely to be struck and silenced by a stranger. The alertness of these little dogs means that they are constantly "on the button," and they can serve you well by really spreading the alarm when danger is nearby.

Chihuahuas are companionable and fun to have around and will fit their mood to yours as companions. They love being with you (constantly suits them fine) and are very comfortable to have around, curled up snoozing on your lap or on the sofa as you read,

184

watch television, write, or whatever. They are as full of mischief as any terrier, like playing games, and love children. A word of caution on the latter subject, though! These are tiny dogs with small, fragile bones which can be easily broken. So do be aware that a child before being permitted to own or play with a Chihuahua *must* be taught to treat it with gentleness as rough games may result in its being really hurt and seriously injured. They are so game and full of fire that one sometimes forgets how small and fragile they are—so do, please, always impress upon any child anticipating enjoying the pleasures of one to be careful and to handle the little dog *with gentleness*.

A Chihuahua can open many doors to pleasure for you. First of all, they are super-intelligent, smart little dogs and if you enjoy training and working with your dog you will find that you have an excellent chance of turning it into an obedience "star."

Then there is the challenge of showing your dog in the conformation classes. Almost anyone can show a Chihuahua, as they are gaited at a normal walking speed in the ring and examined on the table, so those who do not relish galloping around the ring as is a must with many big breeds, or crawling around on the ground "setting up" the dog in mud, gravel, on concrete, tanbark, etc., still can present the dog properly without undue strain or effort on your own part. This makes it more fun for all but the very nimble, athletic, and youthful exhibitors.

Chihuahuas are fun dogs for children to work with in Junior Showmanship, too, as they are a size easy to control and not hard for a youngster to place and set up on the examination table.

Well, I guess I've made my point! Which is that anyone who wants a dog who is very little trouble and lots of pleasure, who is tiny yet has all the best attributes of a big dog, will find certainly a Chihuahua is ideal for *you*.

This is Chico, Mignon Murray's principal stud dog in the mid-1950s who sired many important winners and quality dogs for her. Mignon's Chihuahuas are now located in Jacksonville, Florida.

Chapter 10

The Purchase of Your Chihuahua

Careful consideration should be given to what breed of dog you wish to own prior to your purchase of one. If several breeds are attractive to you, and you are undecided as to which you prefer, learn all you can about the characteristics of each before making your decision. As you do so, you are thus preparing yourself to make an intelligent choice; and this is very important when buying a dog who will be, with reasonable luck, a member of your household for at least a dozen years or more. Obviously since you are reading this book, you have decided on the breed—so now all that remains is to make a good choice.

It is never wise to just rush out and buy the first cute puppy who catches your eye. Whether you wish a dog to show, one with whom to compete in obedience, or one as a family dog purely for his (or her) companionship, the more time and thought you invest as you plan the purchase, the more likely you are to meet with complete satisfaction. The background and early care behind your pet will reflect in the dog's future health and temperament. Even if you are planning the purchase purely as a pet, with no thoughts of showing or breeding in the dog's or puppy's future, it is essen-

187

tial that if the dog is to enjoy a trouble-free future you assure yourself of a healthy, properly raised puppy or adult from sturdy, well-bred stock.

Throughout the pages of this book you will find the names and locations of many well-known and well-established kennels in various areas. Another source of information is the American Kennel Club (51 Madison Avenue, New York, New York 10010) from whom you can obtain a list of recognized breeders in the vicinity of your home. If you plan to have your dog campaigned by a professional handler, by all means let the handler help you locate and select a good dog. Through their numerous clients, handlers have access to a variety of interesting show prospects; and the usual arrangement is that the handler re-sells the dog to you for what his cost has been, with the agreement that the dog be campaigned for you by him throughout the dog's career. It is most strongly recommended that prospective purchasers follow these suggestions, as you thus will be better able to locate and select a satisfactory puppy or dog.

Your first step in searching for your puppy is to make appointments at kennels specializing in your breed, where you can visit and inspect the dogs, both those available for sale and the kennel's basic breeding stock. You are looking for an active, sturdy puppy with bright eyes and intelligent expression and who is friendly and alert; avoid puppies who are hyperactive, dull, or listless. The coat should be clean and thick, with no sign of parasites. The premises on which he was raised should look (and smell) clean and be tidy, making it obvious that the puppies and their surroundings are in capable hands. Should the kennels featuring the breed you intend owning be sparse in your area or not have what you consider attractive, do not hesitate to contact others at a distance and purchase from them if they seem better able to supply a puppy or dog who will please you *so long as it is a recognized breeding kennel of that breed*. Shipping dogs is a regular practice nowadays, with comparatively few problems when one considers the number of dogs shipped each year. A reputable, well-known breeder wants the customer to be satisfied; thus he will represent the puppy fairly. Should you not be pleased with the puppy upon arrival, a breeder such as described will almost certainly permit its return. A conscientious breeder takes real interest and concern in the welfare of the dogs he or she causes to be brought into the world. Such a breeder also is proud of a reputation for integrity. Thus on two counts, for the sake of the dog's future and the breeder's reputation, to such a person a *satisfied* customer takes precedence over a sale at any cost.

If your puppy is to be a pet or "family dog," the earlier the age at which it joins your household the better. Puppies are weaned and ready to start out on their own, under the care of a sensible new owner, at about six weeks old; and if you take a young one, it is often easier to train it to the routine of your household and to your requirements of it than is the case with an older dog which, even though still a puppy technically, may have already started habits you will find difficult to change. The younger puppy is usually less costly, too, as it stands to reason the breeder will not have as much expense invested in it. Obviously, a puppy that has been raised to five or six months old represents more in care and cash expenditure on the breeder's part than one sold earlier and therefore should be and generally is priced accordingly.

There is an enormous amount of truth in the statement that "bargain" puppies seldom turn out to be that. A "cheap" puppy, cheaply raised purely for sale and profit, can and often does lead to great heartbreak including problems and veterinarian's bills which can add up to many times the initial cost of a properly reared dog. On the other hand, just because a puppy is expensive does not assure one that is healthy and well reared. There have been numerous cases where unscrupulous dealers have sold for several hundred dollars puppies that were sickly, in poor condition, and such poor specimens that the breed of which they were supposedly members was barely recognizable. So one cannot always judge a puppy by price alone. Common sense must guide a prospective purchaser, plus the selection of a *reliable*, well-recommended dealer whom you know to have well satisfied customers or, best of all, a specialized breeder. You will probably find the fairest pricing at the kennel of a breeder. Such a person, experienced with the breed in general and with his or her own stock in particular, through extensive association with these dogs has watched enough of them mature to have obviously learned to assess quite accurately each puppy's potential—something impossible where such background is non-existent.

One more word on the subject of pets. Bitches make a fine choice for this purpose as they are usually quieter and more gentle than the males, easier to house train, more affectionate, and less inclined to roam. If you do select a bitch and have no intention of breeding or showing her, by all means have her spayed, for your sake and for hers. The advantages to the owner of a spayed bitch include avoiding the nuisance of "in season" periods which normally occur twice yearly, with the accompanying eager canine swains haunting your premises in an effort to get close to your female, plus the unavoidable messiness and spotting of furniture and rugs at this time, which can be annoying if she is a household companion in the habit of sharing your sofa or bed. As for the spayed bitch, she benefits as she grows older because this simple operation almost entirely eliminates the possibility of breast cancer ever occurring. It is recommended that all bitches eventually be spayed—even those used for show or breeding when their careers have ended—in order that they may enjoy a happier, healthier old age. Please take note, however, that a bitch who has been spayed (or an altered dog) *cannot be shown at American Kennel Club dog shows once this operation has been performed*. Be certain that you are *not* interested in showing her before taking this step.

Also, in selecting a pet, never underestimate the advantages of an older dog, perhaps a retired show dog or a bitch no longer needed for breeding, who may be available quite reasonably priced by a breeder anxious to place such a dog in a loving home. These dogs are settled and can be a delight to own, as they make wonderful companions, especially in a household of adults where raising a puppy can sometimes be a trial.

Everything that has been said about careful selection of your pet puppy and its place of purchase applies, but with many further considerations, when you plan to buy a show dog or foundation stock for a future breeding program. Now is the time for an in-depth study of the breed, starting with every word and every illustration in this book and all others you can find written on the subject. The Standard of the breed now has become your guide, and you must learn not only the words but also how to interpret them and how they are applicable in actual dogs before you are ready to make an intelligent selection of a show dog.

If you are thinking in terms of a dog to show, obviously you must have learned about dog shows and must be in the habit of attending them. This is fine, but now your activity in this direction should be increased, with your attending every single dog show within a reasonable distance from your home. Much can be learned about a breed at ringside at these events. Talk with the breeders who are exhibiting. Study the dogs they are showing. Watch the judging with concentration, noting each decision made, and attempt to follow the reasoning by which the judge has reached it. Note carefully the attributes of the dogs who win and, for your later use, the manner in which each is presented. Close your ears to the ringside know-it-alls, usually novice owners of only a dog or two and very new to the Fancy, who have only derogatory remarks to make about all that is taking place unless they happen to win. This is the type of exhibitor who "comes and goes" through the Fancy and whose interest is usually of very short duration owing to lack of knowledge and dissatisfaction caused by the failure to recognize the need to learn. You, as a fancier it is hoped will last and enjoy our sport over many future years, should develop independent thinking at this stage; you should learn to draw your own conclusions about the merits, or lack of them, seen before you in the ring and, thus, sharpen your own judgement in preparation for choosing wisely and well.

Note carefully which breeders campaign winning dogs, not just an occasional isolated good one but consistent, homebred winners. It is from one of these people that you should select your own future "star."

If you are located in an area where dog shows take place only occasionally or where there are long travel distances involved, you will need to find another testing ground for your ability to select a worthy show dog. Possibly, there are some representative kennels raising this breed within a reasonable distance. If so, by all means ask permission of the owners to visit the kennels and do so when permission is granted. You may not necessarily buy then and there, as they may not have available what you are seeking that very day, but you will be able to see the type of dog being raised there and to discuss the dogs with the breeder. Every time you do this, you add to your knowledge. Should one of these kennels have dogs which especially appeal to you, perhaps you could re-serve a show-prospect puppy from a coming litter. This is fre-quently done, and it is often worth waiting for a puppy, unless you have seen a dog with which you truly are greatly impressed and which is immediately available.

The purchase of a puppy has already been discussed. Obviously this same approach applies in a far greater degree when the pur-chase involved is a future show dog. The only place at which to purchase a show prospect is from a breeder who raises show-type stock; otherwise, you are almost certainly doomed to disappoint-ment as the puppy matures. Show and breeding kennels obviously cannot keep all of their fine young stock. An active breeder-exhib-itor is, therefore, happy to place promising youngsters in the hands of people also interested in showing and winning with them, doing so at a fair price according to the quality and pros-pects of the dog involved. Here again, if no kennel in your imme-diate area has what you are seeking, do not hesitate to contact top breeders in other areas and to buy at long distance. Ask for pic-tures, pedigrees, and a complete description. Heed the breeder's advice and recommendations, after truthfully telling exactly what your expectations are for the dog you purchase. Do you want something with which to win just a few ribbons now and then? Do you want a dog who can complete his championship? Are you thinking of the real "big time" (*i.e.*, seriously campaigning with Best of Breed, Group wins, and possibly even Best in Show as your eventual goal)? Consider it all carefully in advance; then hon-estly discuss your plans with the breeder. You will be better satis-fied with the results if you do this, as the breeder is then in the best position to help you choose the dog who is most likely to come through for you. A breeder selling a show dog is just as anx-ious as the buyer for the dog to succeed, and the breeder will rep-resent the dog to you with truth and honesty. Also, this type of breeder does not lose interest the moment the sale has been made but when necessary will be right there ready to assist you with beneficial advice and suggestions based on years of experience.

As you make inquiries of at least several kennels, keep in mind that show-prospect puppies are less expensive than mature show dogs, the latter often costing close to four figures, and sometimes more. The reason for this is that, with a puppy, there is always an

One of the handsome Smooth Chihuahuas typical of her strain owned by Mignon Murray, Mignon's Chihuahuas, Jacksonville, Florida.

element of chance, the possibility of its developing unexpected faults as it matures or failing to develop the excellence and quality that earlier had seemed probable. There definitely is a risk factor in buying a show-prospect puppy. Sometimes all goes well, but occasionally the swan becomes an ugly duckling. Reflect on this as you consider available puppies and young adults. It just might be a good idea to go with a more mature, though more costly, dog if one you like is available.

When you buy a mature show dog, "what you see is what you get," and it is not likely to change beyond coat and condition which are dependent on your care. Also advantageous for a novice owner is the fact that a mature dog of show quality almost certainly will have received show-ring training and probably match-show experience, which will make your earliest handling ventures far easier.

Frequently it is possible to purchase a beautiful dog who has completed championship but who, owing to similarity in bloodlines, is not needed for the breeder's future program. Here you have the opportunity of owning a champion, usually in the two-to-five-year-old range, which you can enjoy campaigning as a special (for Best of Breed competition) and which will be a settled, handsome dog for you and your family to enjoy with pride.

If you are planning foundation for a future kennel, concentrate on acquiring one or two really superior bitches. These need not necessarily be top show-quality, but they should represent your breed's finest producing bloodlines from a strain noted for producing quality, generation after generation. A proven matron who is already the dam of show-type puppies is, of course, the ideal selection; but these are usually difficult to obtain, no one being anxious to part with so valuable an asset. You just might strike it lucky, though, in which case you are off to a flying start. If you cannot find such a matron available, select a young bitch of finest background from top-producing lines who is herself of decent type, free of obvious faults, and of good quality.

Great attention should be paid to the pedigree of the bitch from whom you intend to breed. If not already known to you, try to see the sire and dam. It is generally agreed that someone starting with a breed should concentrate on a fine collection of topflight bitches and raise a few litters from these before considering keeping one's own stud dog. The practice of buying a stud and then breeding everything you own or acquire to that dog does not always work out well. It is better to take advantage of the many noted sires who are available to be used at stud, who represent all of the leading strains, and in each case to carefully select the one who in type and pedigree seems most compatible to each of your bitches, at least for your first several litters.

To summarize, if you want a "family dog" as a companion, it is best to buy it young and raise it according to the habits of your household. If you are buying a show dog, the more mature it is, the more certain you can be of its future beauty. If you are buying foundation stock for a kennel, then bitches are better, but they must be from the finest *producing* bloodlines.

When you buy a pure-bred dog that you are told is eligible for registration with the American Kennel Club, you are entitled to receive from the seller an application form which will enable you to register your dog. If the seller cannot give you the application form you should demand and receive an identification of your dog consisting of the name of the breed, the registered names and numbers of the sire and dam, the name of the breeder, and your dog's date of birth. If the litter of which your dog is a part is already recorded with the American Kennel Club, then the litter number is sufficient identification.

Do not be misled by promises of papers at some later date. Demand a registration application form or proper identification as described above. If neither is supplied, do not buy the dog. So warns the American Kennel Club, and this is especially important in the purchase of show or breeding stock.

These two Chihuahuas are Goldenbay Moonglow of Hack Pack (*left*);and Goldenbay's Look At Me Hack (*right*), both by the Best in Show winning Ch. Elh Mighty Lunar of Dartan ex Ch. Hack's Pack Velvet Imp. Owned by Golden Bay Chihuahuas, Pat and Bob Porreca, Pleasanton, California.

Chapter 11

The Care of Your Chihuahua Puppy

PREPARING FOR YOUR PUPPY'S ARRIVAL

The moment you decide to be the new owner of a puppy is not one second too soon to start planning for the puppy's arrival in your home. Both the new family member and you will find the transition period easier if your home is geared in advance of the arrival.

The first things to be prepared are a bed for the puppy and a place where you can pen him up for rest periods. Every dog should have a crate of its own from the very beginning, so that he will come to know and love it as his special place where he is safe and happy. It is an ideal arrangement, for when you want him to be free, the crate stays open. At other times you can securely latch it and know that the pup is safely out of mischief. If you travel with him, his crate comes along in the car; and, of course, in traveling by plane there is no alternative but to have a carrier for the dog. If you show your dog, you will want him upon occasion to be in a crate a good deal of the day. So from every consideration, a crate is a very sensible and sound investment in your puppy's future safety and happiness and for your own peace of mind.

The crates most desirable are the wooden ones with removable side panels, which are ideal for cold weather (with the panels in place to keep out drafts) and in hot weather (with the panels removed to allow better air circulation). Wire crates are all right in the summer, but they give no protection from cold or drafts. Aluminum crates, due to the manner in which the metal reflects surrounding temperatures, are not recommended. If it is cold, so is the metal of the crate; if it is hot, the crate becomes burning hot.

When you choose the puppy's crate, be certain that it is roomy enough not to become outgrown. The crate should have sufficient height so the dog can stand up in it as a mature dog and sufficient area so that he can stretch out full length when relaxed. When the puppy is young, first give him shredded newspaper as a bed; the papers can be replaced with a mat or turkish towels when the dog is older. Carpet remnants are great for the bottom of the crate, as they are inexpensive and in case of accidents can be quite easily replaced. As the dog matures and is past the chewing age, a pillow or blanket in the crate is an appreciated comfort.

Sharing importance with the crate is a safe area in which the puppy can exercise and play. If you are an apartment dweller, a baby's playpen can work out well. If you have a yard, an area where he can be outside in safety should be fenced in prior to the dog's arrival at your home. This area does not need to be huge, but it does need to be made safe and secure. If you are in a suburban area where there are close neighbors, stockade fencing works out best as then the neighbors are less aware of the dog and the dog cannot see and bark at everything passing by. If you are out in the country where no problems with neighbors are likely to occur, then regular chain-link fencing is fine. For added precaution in both cases, use a row of concrete blocks or railroad ties inside against the entire bottom of the fence; this precludes or at least considerably lessens the chances of your dog digging his way out.

Be advised that if yours is a single dog, it is very unlikely that it will get sufficient exercise just sitting in the fenced area, which is what most of them do when they are there alone. Two or more dogs will play and move themselves around, but one by itself does little more than make a leisurely tour once around the area to check things over and then lie down. You must include a daily walk or two in your plans if your puppy is to be rugged and well.

Tiny Mite's Brown Bounce, by Ch. B-Beg's Mittee Koko ex Tiny Mite's Koko Betty Jo, owned by Robert DeJonge, Zeeland, Michigan.

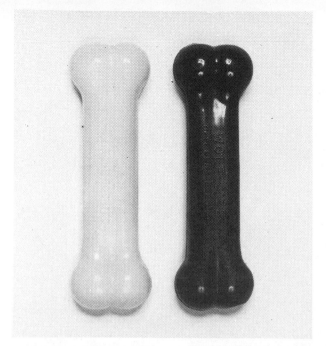

Of the several sizes of Nylabone® that are available, get the petite which is intended for small breeds such as the Chihuahua and other toy dogs. Beside the typical bone shape shown here, Nylabones come in other shapes and flavors, too.

Gumabone® is one other kind of chew toy for all dogs. Gumabones are made of a synthetic material that is flexible yet resistant in character. Like Nylabones, Gumabones come in two flavors and various sizes and shapes (rings, **balls**, wishbones, knots, and others.) Gumabones are toys designed to pro-**vide** dogs with pleasure and exercise.

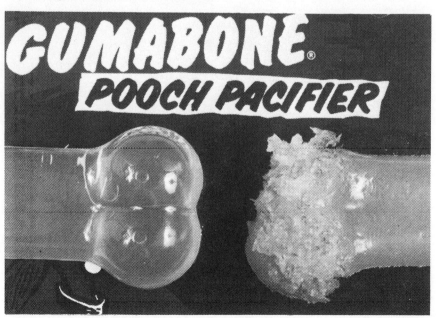

Exercise is extremely important to a puppy's muscular development and to keep a mature dog fit and trim. So make sure that those exercise periods, or walks, a game of ball, and other such activities, are part of your daily program as a dog owner.

If your fenced area has an outside gate, provide a padlock and key and a strong fastening for it, and use them, so that the gate cannot be opened by others and the dog taken or turned free. The ultimate convenience in this regard is, of course, a door (unused for other purposes) from the house around which the fenced area can be enclosed, so that all you have to do is open the door and out into his area he goes. This arrangement is safest of all, as then you need not be using a gate, and it is easier in bad weather since then you can send the dog out without taking him and becoming soaked yourself at the same time. This is not always possible to manage, but if your house is arranged so that you could do it this way, you would never regret it due to the convenience and added safety thus provided. Fencing in the entire yard, with gates to be opened and closed whenever a caller, deliveryman, postman, or some other person comes on your property, really is not safe at all because people not used to gates and their importance are frequently careless about closing and latching gates *securely*. Many heartbreaking incidents have been brought about by someone carelessly only half closing a gate which the owner had thought to be firmly latched and the dog wandering out. For greatest security a fenced *area* definitely takes precedence over a fenced *yard*.

The puppy will need a collar (one that fits now, not one to be grown into) and a lead from the moment you bring him home. Both should be an appropriate weight and type for his size. Also needed are a feeding dish and a water dish, both made preferably of unbreakable material. Your pet supply shop should have an interesting assortment of these and other accessories from which you can choose. Then you will need grooming tools of the type the breeder recommends and some toys. Equally satisfactory is Nylabone®, a nylon bone that does not chip or splinter and that "frizzles" as the puppy chews, providing healthful gum massage. Rawhide chews are safe, too, *if made in the United States*. There was a problem a few years back, owing to the chemicals with which some foreign rawhide toys had been treated. Also avoid plastics and any sort of rubber toys, *particularly those with squeakers* which the puppy may remove and swallow. If you want a ball for the puppy to use when playing with him, select one of very hard construction made for this purpose and do not leave it alone with him because he may chew off and swallow bits of the rubber. Take the ball with you when the game is over. This also applies to some of those "tug of war" type rubber toys which are fun when used with the two of you for that purpose but again should *not* be left behind for the dog to work on with his teeth. Bits of swallowed rubber, squeakers, and other such foreign articles can wreak great havoc in the intestinal tract—do all you can to guard against them.

Too many changes all at once can be difficult for a puppy. For at least the first few days he is with you, keep him on the food and feeding schedule to which he is accustomed. Find out ahead of time from the breeder what he feeds his puppies, how frequently, and at what times of the day. Also find out what, if any, food supplements the breeder has been using and recommends. Then be prepared by getting in a supply of the same food so that you will have it there when you bring the puppy home. Once the puppy is accustomed to his new surroundings, then you can switch the type of food and schedule to fit your convenience, but for the first several days do it as the puppy expects.

Your selection of a veterinarian also should be attended to before the puppy comes home, because you should stop at the vet's office for the puppy to be checked over as soon as you leave the breeder's premises. If the breeder is from your area, ask him for recommendations. Ask you dog-owning friends for their opinions of the local veterinarians, and see what their experiences with those available have been. Choose someone whom several of your friends recommend highly, then contact him about your puppy, perhaps making an appointment to stop in at his office. If the premises are clean, modern, and well equipped, and if you like the veterinarian, make an appointment to bring the puppy in on the day of purchase. Be sure to obtain the puppy's health record from the breeder, including information on such things as shots and worming that the puppy has had.

JOINING THE FAMILY

Remember that, exciting and happy an occasion as it is for you, the puppy's move from his place of birth to your home can be, for him, a traumatic experience. His mother and littermates will be

Ch. Okatoma's Little Bita Whiskey at six and a half months. Already well on the way to championship! Bred, owned, and handled by Patricia Lambert, Hattiesburg, Mississippi.

Ch. Shinybrook Pompeii Pantero, by Ch. Pittore's Pompeii Pan ex Shinybrook Bleuette, was Winners Dog at the 1979 Specialty of the Chihuahua Club of New York.

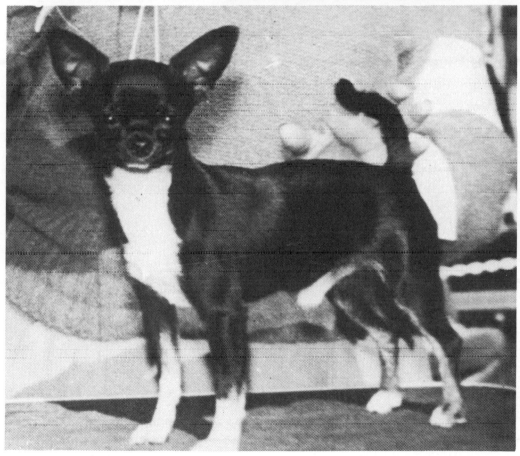

missed. He quite likely will be awed or frightened by the change of surroundings. the person on whom he depended will be gone. Everything should be planned to make his arrival at your home pleasant—to give him confidence and to help him realize that yours is a pretty nice place to be after all.

Never bring a puppy home on a holiday. There just is too much going on with people and gifts and excitement. If he is in honor of an "occasion," work it out so that his arrival will be a few days earlier, or perhaps even better, a few days later than the "occasion." Then your home will be back to it normal routine and the puppy can enjoy your undivided attention. Try not to bring the puppy home in the evening. Early morning is the ideal time, as then he has the opportunity of getting acquainted and the initial strangeness should wear off before bedtime. You will find it a more peaceful night that way. Allow the puppy to investigate as he likes, under your watchful eye. If you already have a pet in the household, keep a careful watch that the relationship between the two gets off to a friendly start or you may quickly find yourself with a lasting problem. Much of the future attitude of each toward the other will depend on what takes place that first day, so keep your mind on what they are doing and let your other activities slide for the moment. Be careful not to let your older pet become jealous by paying more attention to the puppy than to him, as that will start a bad situation immediately.

If you have a child, here again it is important that the relationship start out well. Before the puppy is brought home, you should have a talk with the youngster about puppies so that it will be clearly understood that puppies are fragile and can easily be injured; therefore, they should not be teased, hurt, mauled, or overly rough-housed. A puppy is not an inanimate toy; it is a living thing with a right to be loved and handled respectfully, treatment which will reflect in the dog's attitude toward your child as both mature together. Never permit your children's playmates to mishandle the puppy, tormenting the puppy until it turns on the children in self-defense. Children often do not realize how rough is too rough. You, as a responsible adult, are obligated to assure that your puppy's relationships with children is a pleasant one.

Do not start out by spoiling your puppy. A puppy is usually pretty smart and can be quite demanding. What you had considered to be "just for tonight" may be accepted by the puppy as "for keeps." Be firm with him, strike a routine, and stick to it. The puppy will learn more quickly this way, and everyone will be happier at the result. A radio playing softly or a dim night light are often comforting to a puppy as it gets accustomed to new surroundings and should be provided in preference to bring the puppy to bed with you—unless, of course, you intend him to share the bed as a permanent arrangement.

SOCIALIZING AND TRAINING

Socialization and training of your puppy should start the very day of his arrival in your home. Never address him without calling him by name. A short, simple name is the easiest to teach as it catches the dog's attention quickly, so avoid elaborate call names. Always address the dog by the same name, not a whole series of pet names; the latter will only confuse the puppy.

Use his name clearly, and call the puppy over to you when you see him awake and wandering about. When he comes, make a big fuss over him for being such a good dog. He thus will quickly associate the sound of his name with coming to you and a pleasant happening.

Several hours after the puppy's arrival is not too soon to start accustoming him to the feel of a light collar. He may hardly notice it; or he may struggle, roll over, and try to rub it off his neck with his paws. Divert his attention when this occurs by offering a tasty snack or a toy (starting a game with him) or by petting him. Before long he will have accepted the strange feeling around his neck and no longer appear aware of it. Next comes the lead. Attach it and then immediately take the puppy outside or otherwise try to divert his attention with things to see and sniff. He may struggle against the lead at first, biting at it and trying to free himself. Do not pull him with it at this point; just hold the end loosely and try to follow him if he starts off in any direction. Normally his attention will soon turn to investigating his sourroundings if he is outside or you have taken him into an unfamiliar room in your house; curiosity will take over and he will become interested in sniffing around the surroundings. Just follow him with the lead slackly held until he seems to have completely forgotten about it; then try with gentle urging to get him to follow you. Don't be rough or jerk at him; just tug gently on the lead in short quick motions (steady pulling can become a battle of wills), repeating his name or trying to get him to follow your hand which is holding a bite of food or an interesting toy. If you have an older lead-trained dog, then it should be a cinch to get the puppy to follow along after *him*. In any event the average puppy learns quite quickly and will soon be trotting along nicely on the lead. Once that point has been reached, the next step is to teach him to follow on your left side, or heel. Of course this will not likely be accomplished all in one day but should be done with short training periods over the course of several days until you are satisfied with the result.

During the course of house training your puppy, you will need to take him out frequently and at regular intervals: first thing in the morning directly from the crate, immediately after meals, after the puppy has been napping, or when you notice that the puppy is looking for a spot. Choose more or less the same place to take the puppy each time so that a pattern will be established. If he does not go immediately, do not return him to the house as he will probably relieve himself the moment he is inside. Stay out with him until he has finished; then be lavish with your praise for his good behavior. If you catch the puppy having an accident indoors, grab him firmly and rush him outside, sharply saying "No!" as you pick him up. If you do not see the accident occur, there is little point in doing anything except cleaning it up, as once it has happened and been forgotten, the puppy will most likely not even realize why you are scolding him.

Especially if you live in a big city or are away many hours at a time, having a dog that is trained to go on paper has some very definite advantages. To do this, one proceeds pretty much the same way as taking the puppy outdoors, except now you place the puppy on the newspaper at the proper time. The paper should always be kept in the same spot. An easy way to paper train a puppy if you have a playpen for it or an exercise pen is to line the area with newspapers; then gradually, every day or so, remove a section of newspaper until you are down to just one or two. The puppy acquires the habit of using the paper; and as the prepared area grows smaller, in the majority of cases the dog will continue to use whatever paper is still available. It is pleasant, if the dog is alone for an excessive length of time, to be able to feel that if he needs it the paper is there and will be used.

Lee Lee Pratt showing off her just received Christmas gift. Owned by R.T. Dampson. Bred by Dorothy A. Pratt, Lakeland, Florida.

Glindale's Kipper, Long Coat bitch, proves her diminutive size as she sits alongside a cigarette pack. One of the Chihuahuas from Linda M. Glenn's kennel at Harrington Park, New Jersey.

Ch. Cobtown Begonia, by Ch. Hurd's Kojak ex Cobtown Sweetie Pie, was a top contender in the late 1970s and early 1980s. Winners Bitch from puppy classes at Chihuahua Club of America Specialty. Winner of five Toy Groups and Best of Breed at several Specialties. Bred by John Rhoten and Bob Ulip. Co-owned and handled by Marie Hurd, Council Bluffs, Iowa.

The puppy should form the habit of spending a certain amount of time in his crate, even when you are home. Sometimes the puppy will do this voluntarily, but if not, he should be taught to do so, which is accomplished by leading the puppy over by his collar, gently pushing him inside, and saying firmly, "Down" or "Stay." Whatever expression you use to give a command, stick to the very same one each time for each act. Repetition is the big thing in training—and so is association with what the dog is expected to do. When you mean "Sit" always say exactly that. "Stay" should mean *only* that the dog should remain where he receives the command. "Down" means something else again. Do not confuse the dog by shuffling the commands, as this will create training problems for you.

As soon as he had had his immunization shots, take your puppy with you whenever and wherever possible. There is nothing that will build a self-confident, stable dog like socialization, and it is extremely important that you plan and give the time and energy necessary for this whether your dog is to be a show dog or a pleasant, well-adjusted family member. Take your puppy in the car so that he will learn to enjoy riding and not become carsick as dogs may do if they are infrequent travelers. Take him anywhere you are going where you are certain he will be welcome: visiting friends and relative (if they do not have housepets who may resent the visit), busy shopping centers (keeping him always on lead), or just walking around the streets of your town. If someone admires him (as always seems to happen when one is out with puppies), encourage the stranger to pet and talk with him. Socialization of this type brings out the best in your puppy and helps him to grow up with a friendly outlook, liking the world and its inhabitants. The worst thing that can be done to a puppy's personality is to overly shelter him. By always keeping him at home away from things and people unfamiliar to him you may be creating a personality problem for the mature dog that will be a cross for you to bear later on.

FEEDING YOUR DOG

Time was when providing nourishing food for dogs involved a far more complicated procedure than people now feel is necessary. The old school of thought was that the daily ration must consist of fresh beef, vegetables, cereal, egg yolks, and cottage cheese as basics with such additions as brewer's yeast and vitamin tablets on a daily basis.

During recent years, however, many minds have changed regarding this procedure. Eggs, cottage cheese, and supplements to the diet are still given, but the basic method of feeding dogs has changed; and the change has been, in the opinion of many authorities, definitely for the better. The school of thought now is that you are doing your dogs a favor when you feed them some of the fine commercially prepared dog foods in preference to your own home-cooked concoctions.

The reason behind this new outlook is easily understandable. The dog food industry has grown to be a major one, participated in by some of the best known and most respected names in America. These trusted firms, it is agreed, turn out excellent products, so people are feeding their dog food preparations with confidence and the dogs are thriving, living longer, happier, and healthier lives than ever before. What more could one want?

There are at least half a dozen absolutely top-grade dry foods to be mixed with broth or water and served to your dog according to directions. There are all sorts of canned meats, and there are several kinds of "convenience foods," those in a packet which you open and dump out into the dog's dish. It is just that simple. The convenience foods are neat and easy to use when you are away from home, but generally speaking a dry food mixed with hot water (or soup) and meat is preferred. It is the opinion of many that the canned meat, with its added fortifiers, is more beneficial to the dogs than the fresh meat. However, the two can be alternated or, if you prefer and your dog does well on it, by all means use fresh ground beef. A dog enjoys changes in the meat part of his diet, which is easy with the canned food since all sorts of beef are available (chunk, ground, stewed, and so on), plus lamb, chicken, and even such concoctions as liver and egg, plain liver flavor, and a blend of five meats.

There is also prepared food geared to every age bracket of your dog's life, from puppyhood on through old age, with special additions or modifications to make it particularly nourishing and beneficial. Previous generations never had it so good where the canine dinner is concerned, because these commercially prepared foods are tasty and geared to meeting the dog's gastronomic approval.

Additionally, contents and nutrients are clearly listed on the labels, as are careful instructions for feeding just the right amount for the size, weight, and age of each dog.

With these foods the addition of extra vitamins is not necessary, but if you prefer there are several kinds of those, too, that serve as taste treats as well as being beneficial. Your pet supplier has a full array of them.

Of course there is no reason not to cook up something for your dog if you would feel happier doing so. But it seems unnecessary when such truly satisfactory rations are available with so much less trouble and expense.

How often you feed your dog is a matter of how it works out best for you. Many owners prefer to do it once a day. It is generally agreed that two meals, each of smaller quantity, are better for the digestion and more satisfying to the dog, particularly if yours is a household member who stands around and watches preparations for the family meals. Do not overfeed. This is the shortest route to all sorts of problems. Follow directions and note carefully how your dog is looking. If your dog is overweight, cut back the quantity of food a bit. If the dog looks thin, then increase the amount. Each dog is an individual and the food intake should be adjusted to his requirements to keep him feeling and looking trim and in top condition.

From the time puppies are fully weaned until they are about twelve weeks old, they should be fed four times daily. From three months to six months of age, three meals should suffice. At six months of age the puppies can be fed two meals, and the twice daily feedings can be continued until the puppies are close to one year old, at which time feeding can be changed to once daily if desired. If you do feed just once a day, do so by early afternoon at the latest and give the dog a snack, a biscuit or two, at bedtime.

Remember that plenty of fresh water should always be available to your puppy or dog for drinking. This is of utmost importance to his health.

Ch. Quachitah For Your Eyes Only moves smartly around the Toy Group ring at Westminster 1984, showing off the style which helped him to leave that ring the winner. Bred, owned, and handled by Linda George, Waukesha, Wisconsin.

Chapter 12

The Making of a Show Dog

If you have decided to become a show dog exhibitor, you have accepted a very real and very exciting challenge. The groundwork has been accomplished with the selection of your future show prospect. If you have purchased a puppy, it is assumed that you have gone through all the proper preliminaries concerning good care, which should be the same if the puppy is a pet or future show dog, with a few added precautions for the latter.

GENERAL CONSIDERATIONS

Remember the importance of keeping your future winner in trim, top condition. Since you want him neither too fat nor too thin, his appetite for his proper diet should be guarded, and children and guests should not be permitted to constantly feed him "goodies." The best treat of all is a small wad of raw ground beef or a packaged dog treat. To be avoided are ice cream, cake, cookies, potato chips, and other fattening items which will cause the dog to put on weight and may additionally spoil his appetite for the proper, nourishing, well-balanced diet so essential to good health and condition.

The importance of temperament and showmanship cannot possibly be overestimated. They have put many a mediocre dog across, while lack of them can ruin the career of an otherwise outstanding specimen. From the day your dog joins your family, socialize him. Keep him accustomed to being with people and to being handled by people. Encourage your friends and relatives to "go over" him as the judges will in the ring so this will not seem a strange and upsetting experience. Practice showing his "bite" (the manner in which his teeth meet) quickly and deftly. It is quite simple to slip the lips apart with your fingers, and the puppy should be willing to accept this from you or the judge without struggle.

Some judges prefer that the exhibitors display the dog's bite and other mouth features themselves. These are the considerate ones, who do not wish to chance the spreading of possible infection from dog to dog with their hands on each one's mouth—a courtesy particularly appreciated in these days of virus epidemics. But the old-fashioned judges still persist in doing it themselves, so the dog should be ready for either possibility.

Take your future show dog with you in the car, thus accustoming him to riding so that he will not become carsick on the day of a dog show. He should associate pleasure and attention with going in the car, van, or motor home. Take him where it is crowded: downtown, to the shops, everywhere you go that dogs are permitted. Make the expeditions fun for him by frequent petting and words of praise; do not just ignore him as you go about your errands.

Do not overly shelter your future show dog. Instinctively you may want to keep him at home where he is safe from germs or danger. This can be foolish on two counts. The first reason is that a puppy kept away from other dogs builds up no natural immunity against all the things with which he will come in contact at dog shows, so it is wiser to keep him up-to-date on all protective shots and then let him become accustomed to being among dogs and dog owners. Also, a dog who is never among strange people, in strange places, or among strange dogs may grow up with a shyness or timidity of spirit that will cause you real problems as his show career draws near.

Keep your show prospect's coat in immaculate condition with frequent grooming and daily brushing. When bathing is necessary, use a mild dog shampoo or whatever the breeder of your puppy may suggest. Several of the brand-name products do an excellent job. Be sure to rinse thoroughly so as not to risk skin irritation by traces of soap left behind, and protect against soap entering the eyes by a drop of castor oil in each before you lather up. Use warm water (be sure it is not uncomfortably hot or chillingly cold) and a good spray. Make certain you allow your dog to dry thoroughly in a warm, draft-free area (or outdoors, if it is warm and sunny) so that he doesn't catch cold. Then proceed to groom him to perfection.

Toenails should be watched and trimmed every few weeks. It is important not to permit nails to grow excessively long, as they will ruin the appearance of both the feet and pasterns.

A show dog's teeth must be kept clean and free of tartar. Hard dog biscuits can help toward this, but if tartar accumulates, see that it is removed promptly by your veterinarian. Bones for chewing are not suitable for show dogs as they tend to damage and wear down the tooth enamel.

Assuming that you will be handling the dog yourself, or even if he will be professionally handled, a few moments each day of dog show routine is important. Practice setting him up as you have seen the exhibitors do at the shows you've attended, and teach him to hold this position once you have him stacked to your satisfaction. Make the learning period pleasant by being firm but lavish in your praise when he responds correctly. Teach him to gait at your side at a moderate rate on a loose lead. When you have mastered the basic essentials at home, then hunt out and join a training class for future work. Training classes are sponsored by show-giving clubs in many areas, and their popularity is steadily increasing. If you have no other way of locating one, perhaps your veterinarian would know of one through some of his other clients; but if you are sufficiently aware of the dog show world to want a show dog, you will probably be personally acquainted with other people who will share information of this type with you.

Accustom your show dog to being in a crate (which you should be doing with a pet dog as well). He should relax in his crate at the shows "between times" for his own well being and safety.

MATCH SHOWS

Your show dog's initial experience in the ring should be in match show competition. This type of event is intended as a learning experience for both the dog and the exhibitor. You will not feel embarrassed or out of place no matter how poorly your puppy may behave or how inept your attempts at handling may be, as you will find others there with the same type of problems. The important thing is that you get the puppy out and into a show ring where the two of you can practice together and learn the ropes.

Only on rare occasions is it necessary to make match show entries in advance, and even those with a pre-entry policy will usually accept entries at the door as well. Thus you need not plan several weeks ahead, as is the case with point shows, but can go when the mood strikes you. Also there is a vast difference in the cost, as match show entries only cost a few dollars while entry fees for the point shows may be over ten dollars, an amount none of us needs to waste until we have some idea of how the puppy will behave or how much more pre-show training is needed.

Match shows are frequently judged by professional handlers who, in addition to making the awards, are happy to help new exhibitors with comments and advice on their puppies and their presentation of them. Avail yourself of all these opportunities before heading out to the sophisticated world of the point shows.

POINT SHOWS

As previously mentioned, entries for American Kennel Club point shows must be made in advance. This must be done on an official entry blank of the show-giving club. The entry must then be filed either personally or by mail with the show superintendent or the show secretary (if the event is being run by the club members alone and a superintendent has not been hired, this information will appear on the premium list) in time to reach its destination prior to the published closing date or filling of the quota. These entries must be made carefully, must be signed by the owner of the dog or the owner's agent (your professional handler), and must be accompanied by the entry fee; otherwise they will not be accepted. Remember that it is not when the entry leaves your hands that counts, but the date of arrival at its destination. If you are relying on the mails, which are not always dependable, get the entry off well before the deadline to avoid disappointment.

The noted Best in Show winner, Ch. Elh's Mighty Lunar of Dartan handled by Michael Diaz for owner Pat Porreca, Pleasanton, California, winning the Toy Group at Rogue Valley K.C. in 1983.

Chihuahua Club of Metropolitan New York Specialty Show in June 1960. The author is judging, and had just awarded Winners Bitch to the beautiful bitch, Princess, handled by Mamie Crouse. Princess completed her championship with ease, going on to some splendid winning as a special as she was widely admired.

A dog must be entered at a dog show in the name of the actual owner at the time of the entry closing date of that specific show. If a registered dog has been acquired by a new owner, it must be entered in the name of the new owner in any show for which entries close after the date of acquirement, regardless of whether the new owner has or has not actually received the registration certificate indicating that the dog is recorded in his name. State on the entry form whether or not transfer application has been mailed to the American Kennel Club, and it goes without saying that the latter should be attended to promptly when you purchase a registered dog.

In filling out your entry blank, type, print, or write clearly, paying particular attention to the spelling of names, correct registration numbers, and so on. Also, if there is more than one variety in your breed, be sure to indicate into which category your dog is being entered.

The **Puppy Class** is for dogs or bitches who are six months of age and under twelve months and who are not champions. The age of a dog shall be calculated up to and inclusive of the first day of a show. For example, the first day a dog whelped on January 1st is eligible to compete in a Puppy Class at a show is July 1st of the same year; and he may continue to compete in Puppy Classes up to and including a show on December 31 of the same year, but he is *not* eligible to compete in a Puppy Class at a show held on or after January 1 of the following year.

The Puppy Class is the first one in which you should enter your puppy. In it a certain allowance will be made for the fact that they *are* puppies, thus an immature dog or one displaying less than perfect showmanship will be less severely penalized than, for instance, would be the case in Open. It is also quite likely that others in the class will be suffering from these problems, too. When you enter a puppy, be sure to check the classification with care, as some shows divide their Puppy Class into a 6-9 months old section and a 9-12 months old section.

The **Novice Class** is for dogs six months of age and over, whelped in the United States or Canada, who *prior to the official closing date for entries* have *not* won three first prizes in the Novice Class, any first prize at all in the Bred-by-Exhibitor, American-bred, or Open Classes, or one or more points toward championship. The provisions for this class are confusing to many people, which is probably the reason exhibitors do not enter in it more frequently. A dog may win any number of first prizes in the Puppy Class and still retain his eligibility for Novice. He may place second, third, or fourth not only in Novice on an unlimited number of occasions, but also in Bred-by-Exhibitor, American-bred and Open and still remain eligible for Novice. But he may no longer be shown in Novice when he has won three blue ribbons in that class, when he has won even one blue ribbon in either Bred-by-Exhibitor, American-bred, or Open, or when he has won a single championship point.

In determining whether or not a dog is eligible for the Novice Class, keep in mind the fact that previous wins are calculated according to the official published date for closing of entries, not by the date on which you may actually have made the entry. So if in the interim, between the time you made the entry and the official closing date, your dog makes a win causing him to become ineligible for Novice, change your class *immediately* to another for which he will be eligible, preferably either Bred-by-Exhibitor or American-bred. To do this, you must contact the show's superintendent or secretary, at first by telephone to save time and then in writing to confirm it. The Novice Class always seems to have the fewest entries of any class, and therefore it is a splendid "practice ground" for you and your young dog while you are getting the "feel" of being in the ring.

Bred-by-Exhibitor Class is for dogs whelped in the United States or, if individually registered in the American Kennel Club Stud Book, for dogs whelped in Canada who are six months of age or older, are not champions, and are owned wholly or in part by the person or by the spouse of the person who was the breeder or one of the breeders of record. Dogs entered in this class must be handled in the class by an owner or by a member of the immediate family of the owner. Members of an immediate family for this purpose are husband, wife, father, mother, son, daughter, brother, or sister. This is the class which is really the "breeders' showcase," and the one which breeders should enter with particular pride to show off their achievements.

The **American-bred Class** is for all dogs excepting champions, six months of age or older, who were whelped in the United States by reason of a mating which took place in the United States.

The **Open Class** is for any dog six months of age or older (this is the only restriction for this class). Dogs with championship points compete in it, dogs who are already champions are eligible to do so, dogs who are imported can be entered, and, of course, American-bred dogs compete in it. This class is, for some strange reason, the favorite of exhibitors who are "out to win." They rush to enter their pointed dogs in it, under the false impression that by doing so they assure themselves of greater attention from the judges. This really is not so, and some people feel that to enter in one of the less competitive classes, with a better chance of winning it and thus earning a second opportunity of gaining the judge's approval by returning to the ring in the Winners Class, can often be a more effective strategy.

One does not enter the **Winners Class.** One earns the right to compete in it by winning first prize in Puppy, Novice, Bred-by-Exhibitor, American-bred, or Open. No dog who has been defeated on the same day in one of these classes is eligible to compete for Winners, and every dog who has been a blue-ribbon winner in one of them and not defeated in another, should he have been entered in more than one class (as occasionally happens), *must* do so. Following the selection of the Winners Dog or the Winners Bitch, the dog or bitch receiving that award leaves the ring. Then the dog or bitch who placed second in that class, unless previously beaten by another dog or bitch in another class at the same show, re-enters the ring to compete against the remaining first-prize winners for Reserve. The latter award indicates that the dog or bitch selected for it is standing "in reserve" should the one who received Winners be disqualified or declared ineligible through any technicality when the awards are checked at the American Kennel Club. In that case, the one who placed Reserve is moved up to Winners, at the same time receiving the appropriate championship points.

Winners Dog and Winners Bitch are the awards which carry points toward championship with them. The points are based on the number of dogs or bitches actually in competition, and the points are scaled one through five, the latter being the greatest number available to any one dog or bitch at any one show. Three-, four-, or five-point wins are considered majors. In order to be-

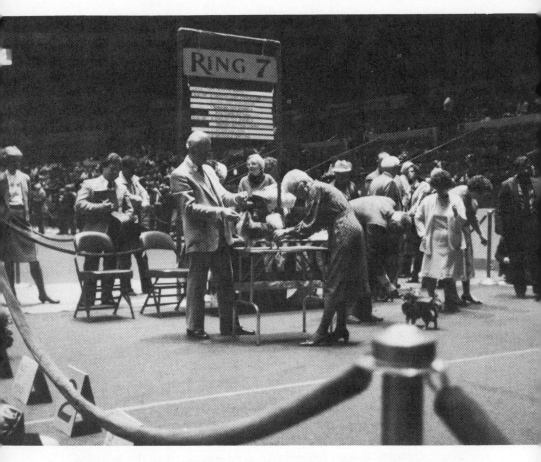

Judging Chihuahuas at Westminster. Note the manner in which the judge is examining the hindquarters, checking hocks and stifle for proper conformation.

Facing page: Glindale's Marmaduke taking Best of Winners at Westminster in 1984 for owner Linda M. Glenn, Glindale Chihuahuas, Harrington Park, New Jersey.

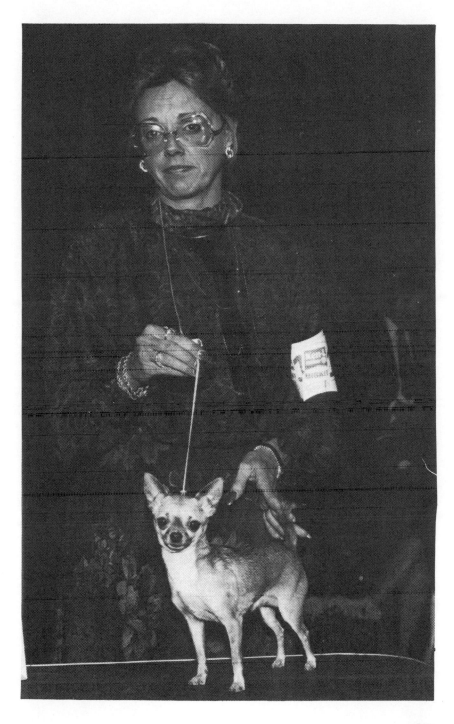

come a champion, a dog or bitch must have won two majors under two different judges, plus at least one point from a third judge, and the additional points necessary to bring the total to fifteen. When your dog has gained fifteen points as described above, a championship certificate will be issued to you, and your dog's name will be published in the champions of record list in the *Pure-Bred Dogs/American Kennel Gazette*, the official publication of the American Kennel Club.

The scale of championship points for each breed is worked out by the American Kennel Club and reviewed annually, at which time the number required in competition may be either changed (raised or lowered) or remain the same. The scale of championship points for all breeds is published annually in the May issue of the *Gazette*, and the current ratings for each breed within that area are published in every show catalog.

When a dog or bitch is adjudged Best of Winners, its championship points are, for that show, compiled on the basis of which sex had the greater number of points. If there are two points in dogs and four in bitches and the dog goes Best of Winners, then *both* the dog and the bitch are awarded an equal number of points, in this case four. Should the Winners Dog or the Winners Bitch go on to win Best of Breed or Best of Variety, additional points are accorded for the additional dogs and bitches defeated by so doing, provided, of course, that there were entries specifically for Best of Breed competition or Specials, as these specific entries are generally called.

If your dog or bitch takes Best of Opposite Sex after going Winners, points are credited according to the number of the same sex defeated in both the regular classes and Specials competition. If Best of Winners is also won, then whatever additional points for each of these awards are available will be credited. Many a one- or two-point win has grown into a major in this manner.

Moving further along, should your dog win its **Variety Group** from the classes (in other words, if it has taken either Winners Dog or Winners Bitch), you then receive points based on the greatest number of points awarded to any member of any breed included within that Group during that show's competition. Should the day's winning also include Best in Show, the same rule of thumb applies, and your dog or bitch receives the highest num-

Ch. Tiny Mite's Diamond Prince handled here by Margaret E. Krause for owners Tiny Mite Chihuahuas, Robert L. DeJonge. Pictured taking Best of Breed at the Detroit Chihuahua Club Specialty, November 1972.

ber of points awarded to any other dog of any breed at that event.

Best of Breed competition consists of the Winners Dog and the Winners Bitch, who automatically compete on the strength of those awards, in addition to whatever dogs and bitches have been entered specifically for this class for which champions of record are eligible. Since July 1980, dogs who, according to their owner's records, have completed the requirements for a championship after the closing of entries for the show (but whose championships

Ch. Hurd's Kojak, by Hurd's Sugar Flake ex Hurd's Molly, is a grandson of Ch. Hurd's Honey Bee and great-grandson of Ch. Hurd' Lil Indian, was the leading stud dog at Hurd's Kennels during the 1970s. Two of his offspring were Best in Show at the Chihuahua Club of America National Specialty Shows (Ch. Hurd Cobtown Red Hot Poker and Champion Cobtown Begonia). Kojak is pictured taking Winners Dog at a Chihuahua Club of America Specialty Show, handled by Marie Hurd, co-breeder-owner with Max Hurd, Council Bluffs, Iowa.

are unconfirmed) may be transferred from one of the regular classes to the Best of Breed competition, provided this transfer is made by the show superintendent or show secretary *prior to the start of any judging at the show*.

This has proved an extremely popular new rule, as under it a dog can finish on Saturday and then be transferred and compete as a Special on Sunday. It must be emphasized that *the change must be made prior to the start of any part of the day's judging, not for just your individual breed*.

In the United States, Best of Breed winners are entitled to compete in the Variety Group which includes them. This is not mandatory; it is a privilege which exhibitors value. (In Canada, Best of Breed winners *must* compete in the Variety Group or they lose any points already won.) The dogs winning *first* in each of the seven Variety Groups *must* compete for Best in Show. Missing the opportunity of taking your dog in for competition in its Group is foolish, as it is there where the general public is most likely to notice your breed and become interested in learning about it.

Non-regular classes are sometimes included at the all-breed shows, and they are almost invariably included at Specialty shows. These include Stud Dog Class and Brood Bitch Class, which are judged on the basis of the quality of the two offspring accompanying the sire or dam. The quality of the latter two is beside the point and should not be considered by the judge; it is the youngsters who count, and the quality of *both* are to be averaged to decide which sire or dam is the best and most consistent producer. Then there is the Brace Class (which, at all-breed shows, moves up to Best Brace in each Variety Group and then Best Brace in Show) which is judged on the similarity and evenness of appearance of the two brace members. In other words, the two dogs should look like identical twins in size, color, and conformation and should move together almost as a single dog, one person handling with precision and ease. The same applies to the Team Class competition, except that four dogs are involved and, if necessary, two handlers.

The Veterans Class is for the older dog, the minimum age of whom is seven years. This class is judged on the quality of the dogs, as the winner competes in Best of Breed competition and has, on a respectable number of occasions, been known to take that top award. So the point is *not* to pick out the oldest dog, as some judges seem to believe, but the best specimen of the breed, exactly as in the regular classes.

Then there are Sweepstakes and Futurity Stakes sponsored by many Specialty clubs, sometimes as part of their regular Specialty shows and sometimes as separate events on an entirely different occasion. The difference between the two stakes is that Sweepstakes entries usually include dogs from six to eighteen months of age with entries made at the same time as the others for the show, while for a Futurity the entries are bitches nominated when bred and the individual puppies entered at or shortly following their birth.

JUNIOR SHOWMANSHIP COMPETITION

If there is a youngster in your family between the ages of ten and sixteen, there is no better or more rewarding hobby than becoming an active participant in Junior Showmanship. This is a marvelous activity for young people. It teaches responsibility, good sportsmanship, the fun of competition where one's own skills are the deciding factor of success, proper care of a pet, and how to socialize with other young folks. Any youngster may experience the thrill of emerging from the ring a winner and the satisfaction of a good job well done.

Entry in Junior Showmanship Classes is open to any boy or girl who is at least ten years old and under seventeen years old on the day of the show. The Novice Junior Showmanship Class is open to youngsters who have not already won, at the time the entries close, three firsts in this class. Youngsters who have won three firsts in Novice may compete in the Open Junior Showmanship Class. Any junior handler who wins his third first-place award in Novice may participate in the Open Class at the same show, provided that the Open Class has at least one other junior handler entered and competing in it that day. The Novice and Open Classes may be divided into Junior and Senior Classes. Youngsters between the ages of ten and twelve, inclusively, are eligible for the Junior division; and youngsters between thirteen and seventeen, inclusively, are eligible for the Senior division.

Any of the foregoing classes may be separated into individual classes for boys and for girls. If such a division is made, it must be so indicated on the premium list. The premium list also indi-

A ringful of Chihuahua celebritites with their dogs at Westminster 1983. Photo courtesy of Linda Glenn.

cates the prize for Best Junior Handler, if such a prize is being offered at the show. Any youngster who wins a first in any of the regular classes may enter the competition for this prize, provided the youngster has been undefeated in any other Junior Showmanship Class at that show.

Junior Showmanship Classes, unlike regular conformation classes in which the quality of the dog is judged, are judged solely on the skill and ability of the junior handling the dog. Which dog is best is not the point—it is which youngster does the best job with the dog that is under consideration. Eligibility requirements for the dog being shown in Junior Showmanship, and other detailed information, can be found in *Regulations for Junior Showmanship*, available from the American Kennel Club.

A junior who has a dog that he or she can enter in both Junior Showmanship and conformation classes has twice the opportunity for success and twice the opportunity to get into the ring and work with the dog, a combination which can lead to not only awards for expert handling, but also, if the dog is of sufficient quality, for making a conformation champion.

PRE-SHOW PREPARATIONS

Preparation of the items you will need as a dog show exhibitor should not be left until the last moment. They should be planned and arranged several days in advance of the show in order for you to remain calm and relaxed as the countdown starts.

The importance of the crate has already been mentioned and should already be part of your equipment. Of equal importance is the grooming table, which very likely you have also already acquired for use at home. You should take it along with you to the shows, as your dog will need last minute touches before entering the ring. Should you have not yet made this purchase, folding tables with rubber tops are made specifically for this purpose and can be purchased at most dog shows, where concession booths with marvelous assortments of "doggy" necessities are to be found, or at your pet supplier. You will also need a sturdy tack box (also available at the dog show concessions) in which to carry your grooming tools and equipment. The latter should include:

Chihuahuas at Westminster! This informal snapshot shows some of the beautiful quality in Long Coats which assemble for this prestigious event. Courtesy of the Mooneys, Rockville, Maryland.

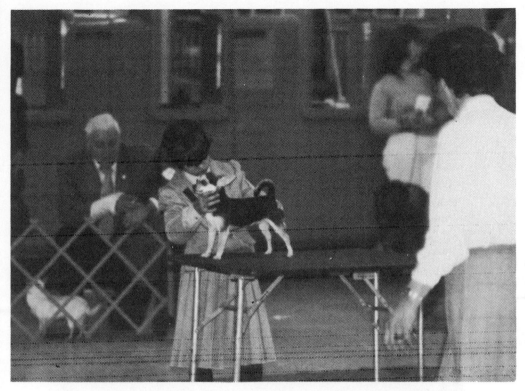

Miss Kristy Glenn carefully sets up "Howard" on the judging table at Meadowlands as Mike Smith, noted professional handler and Chihuahua breeder (now deceased), watches with approval from his vantage point outside the ring.

brushes; combs; scissors; nail clippers; whatever you use for last minute clean-up jobs; cotton swabs; first-aid equipment; and anything you are in the habit of using on the dog, including a leash or two of the type you prefer, some well-cooked and dried-out liver or any of the small packaged "dog treats" for use as bait in the ring, an atomizer in case you wish to dampen your dog's coat when you are preparing him for the ring, and so on. A large turkish towel to spread under the dog on the grooming table is also useful.

Take a large thermos or cooler of ice, the biggest one you can accommodate in your vehicle, for use by "man and beast." Take a jug of water (there are lightweight, inexpensive ones available at all sporting goods shops) and a water dish. If you plan to feed the dog at the show, or if you and the dog will be away from home more than one day, bring food for him from home so that he will have the type to which he is accustomed.

You may or may not have an exercise pen. While the shows do provide areas for exercise of the dogs, these are among the most likely places to have your dog come in contact with any illnesses which may be going around, and having a pen of your own for your dog's use is excellent protection. Such a pen comes in handy while you're travelling; since it is roomier than a crate, it becomes a comfortable place for your dog to relax and move around in, especially when you're at motels or rest stops. These pens are available at the show concession stands and come in a variety of heights and sizes. A set of "pooper scoopers" should also be part of your equipment, along with a package of plastic bags for cleaning up after your dog.

Bring along folding chairs for the members of your party, unless all of you are fond of standing, as these are almost never provided by the clubs. Have your name stamped on the chairs so that there will be no doubt as to whom the chairs belong. Bring whatever you and your family enjoy for drinks or snacks in a picnic basket or cooler, as show food, in general, is expensive and usually not great. You should always have a pair of boots, a raincoat, and a rain hat with you (they should remain permanently in your vehicle if you plan to attend shows regularly), as well as a sweater, a warm coat, and a change of shoes. A smock or big cover-up apron will assure that you remain tidy as you prepare the dog for the ring. Your overnight case should include a small sewing kit for emergency repairs, bandaids, headache and indigestion remedies, and any personal products or medications you normally use.

In your car, you should always carry maps of the area where you are headed and an assortment of motel directories. Generally speaking, Holiday Inns have been found to be the nicest about taking dogs. Ramadas and Howard Johnsons generally do so cheerfully (with a few exceptions). Best Western generally frowns on pets (not always, but often enough to make it necessary to find out which do). Some of the smaller chains welcome pets; the majority of privately-owned motels do not.

Have everything prepared the night before the show to expedite your departure. Be sure that the dog's identification and your judging program and other show information are in your purse or briefcase. If you are taking sandwiches, have them ready. Anything that goes into the car the night before the show will be one thing less to remember in the morning. Decide upon what you will wear and have it out and ready. If there is any question in your mind about what to wear, try on the possibilities before the day of the show; don't risk feeling you may want to change when you see yourself dressed a few moments prior to departure time!

In planning your outfit, make it something simple that will not detract from your dog. Remember that a dark dog silhouettes attractively against a light background and vice-versa. Sport clothes always seem to look best at dog shows, preferably conservative in type and not overly "loud" as you do not want to detract from your dog, who should be the focus of interest at this point. What you wear on your feet is important. Many types of flooring can be hazardously slippery, as can wet grass. Make it a habit to wear rubber soles and low or flat heels in the ring for your own safety, especially if you are showing a dog that likes to move out smartly.

Your final step in pre-show preparation is to leave yourself plenty of time to reach the show that morning. Traffic can get amazingly heavy as one nears the immediate area of the show, finding a parking place can be difficult, and other delays may occur. You'll be in better humor to enjoy the day if your trip to the show is not fraught with panic over fear of not arriving in time!

ENJOYING THE DOG SHOW

From the moment of your arrival at the show until after your dog has been judged, keep foremost in your mind the fact that he is your reason for being there and that he should therefore be the center of your attention. Arrive early enough to have time for those last-minute touches that can make a great difference when he enters the ring. Be sure that he has ample time to exercise and that he attends to personal matters. A dog arriving in the ring and immediately using it as an exercise pen hardly makes a favorable impression on the judge.

When you reach ringside, ask the steward for your arm-card and anchor it firmly into place on your arm. Make sure that you are where you should be when your class is called. The fact that you have picked up your arm-card does not guarantee, as some seem to think, that the judge will wait for you. The judge has a

Terrymont Marsukri the Wiz, by Ch. Harmonies Sounder of Weslyn ex Ch. Pittore's Pazzazite Picante at age six months. Bred by Ruth Terry; owned by A. Mellinger, Matawan, New Jersey.

full schedule which he wishes to complete on time. Even though you may be nervous, assume an air of calm self-confidence. Remember that this is a hobby to be enjoyed, so approach it in that state of mind. The dog will do better, too, as he will be quick to reflect your attitude.

Always show your dog with an air of pride. If you make mistakes in presenting him, don't worry about it. Next time you will do better. Do not permit the presence of more experienced exhibitors to intimidate you. After all, they, too, were once newcomers.

The judging routine usually starts when the judge asks that the dogs be gaited in a circle around the ring. During this period the judge is watching each dog as it moves, noting style, topline, reach and drive, head and tail carriage, and general balance. Keep your mind and your eye on your dog, moving him at his most becoming gait and keeping your place in line without coming too close to the exhibitor ahead of you. Always keep your dog on the inside of the circle, between yourself and the judge, so that the judge's view of the dog is unobstructed.

Calmly pose the dog when requested to set up for examination. If you are at the head of the line and many dogs are in the class, go all the way to the end of the ring before starting to stack the dog, leaving sufficient space for those behind you to line theirs up as well, as requested by the judge. If you are not at the head of the line but between other exhibitors, leave sufficient space ahead of your dog for the judge to examine him. The dogs should be spaced so that the judge is able to move among them to see them from all angles. In practicing to "set up" or "stack" your dog for the judge's examination, bear in mind the importance of doing so quickly and with dexterity. The judge has a schedule to meet and only a few moments in which to evaluate each dog. You will immeasurably help yours to make a favorable impression if you are able to "get it all together" in a minimum amount of time. Practice at home before a mirror can be a great help toward bringing this about, facing the dog so that you see him from the same side that the judge will and working to make him look right in the shortest length of time.

Listen carefully as the judge describes the manner in which the dog is to be gaited, whether it is straight down and straight back; down the ring, across, and back; or in a triangle. The latter has become the most popular pattern with the majority of judges. "In a triangle" means the dog should move down the outer side of the ring to the first corner, across that end of the ring to the second corner, and then back to the judge from the second corner, using the center of the ring in a diagonal line. Please learn to do this pattern without breaking at each corner to twirl the dog around you, a senseless maneuver that has been noticed on occasion. Judges like to see the dog in an uninterrupted triangle, as they are thus able to get a better idea of the dog's gait.

It is impossible to overemphasize that the gait at which you move your dog is tremendously important and considerable study and thought should be given to the matter. At home, have someone move the dog for you at different speeds so that you can tell which shows him off to best advantage. The most becoming action almost invariably is seen at a moderate gait, head up and topline holding. Do not gallop your dog around the ring or hurry him into a speed atypical of his breed. Nothing being rushed appears at its best; give your dog a chance to move along at his (and the breed's) natural gait. For a dog's action to be judged accurately, that dog should move with strength and power, but not excessive speed, holding a straight line as he goes to and from the judge.

As you bring the dog back to the judge, stop him a few feet away and be sure that he is standing in a becoming position. Bait him to show the judge an alert expression, using whatever tasty morsel he has been trained to expect for this purpose or, if that works better for you, use a small squeak-toy in your hand. A reminder, please, to those using liver or treats: take them with you when you leave the ring. Do not just drop them on the ground where they will be found by another dog.

When the awards have been made, accept yours graciously, no matter how you actually may feel about it. What's done is done, and arguing with a judge or stomping out of the ring is useless and a reflection on your sportsmanship. Be courteous, congratulate the winner if your dog was defeated, and try not to show your disappointment. By the same token, please be a gracious winner; this, surprisingly, sometimes seems to be still more difficult.

Facing page: Ch. Quachitah Fire and Ice, all-breed Best in Show winner, bred and owned by Linda George, Waukesha, Wisconsin. Pictured winning Best in Show, all-breeds, at Indianhead K.C. in August 1982.

IN SHOW

HEAD K.C.

ST 28,1982

LSON PHOTO

INDIANHEAD
KENNEL CLUB

Long Coat Chihuahua Ch. Terrymont Trifle Bit of Candy, C.D.X. was bred and owned by Terrymont Kennels, Herbert and Ruth Terry, Weston, Connecticut. A widely respected show and obedience Chihuahua.

Chapter 13

Your Chihuahua and Obedience

For its own protection and safety, every dog should be taught, at the very least, to recognize and obey the commands "Come," "Heel," "Down," "Sit," and "Stay." Doing so at some time might save the dog's life and in less extreme circumstances will certainly make him a better behaved, more pleasant member of society. If you are patient and enjoy working with your dog, study some of the excellent books available on the subject of obedience and then teach your canine friend these basic manners. If you need the stimulus of working with a group, find out where obedience training classes are held (usually your veterinarian, your dog's breeder, or a dog-owning friend can tell you) and you and your dog can join up. Alternatively, you could let someone else do the training by sending the dog to class, but this is not very rewarding because you lose the opportunity of working with your dog and the pleasure of the rapport thus established.

If you are going to do it yourself, there are some basic rules which you should follow. You must remain calm and confident in attitude. Never lose your temper and frighten or punish your dog unjustly. Be quick and lavish with praise each time a command is correctly followed. Make it fun for the dog and he will be eager to please you by responding correctly. Repetition is the keynote, but it should not be continued without recess to the point of tedium. Limit the training sessions to ten- or fifteen-minute periods at a time.

Formal obedience training can be followed, and very frequently is, by entering the dog in obedience competition to work toward an obedience degree, or several of them, depending on the dog's aptitude and your own enjoyment. Obedience trials are held in conjunction with the majority of all-breed conformation dog shows, with Specialty shows, and frequently as separate Specialty events. If you are working alone with your dog, a list of trial dates might be obtained from your dog's veterinarian, your dog breeder, or a dog-owning friend; the AKC *Gazette* lists shows and trials to be scheduled in the coming months; and if you are a member of a training class, you will find the information readily available.

The goals for which one works in the formal AKC Member or Licensed Trials are the following titles: Companion Dog (C.D.), Companion Dog Excellent (C.D.X.), and Utility Dog (U.D.). These degrees are earned by receiving three "legs," or qualifying scores, at each level of competition. The degrees must be earned in order, with one completed prior to starting work on the next. For example, a dog must have earned C.D. prior to starting work on C.D.X.; then C.D.X. must be completed before U.D. work begins. The ultimate title attainable in obedience work is Obedience Trial Champion (O.T.Ch.)

When you see the letters C.D. following a dog's name, you will know that this dog has satisfactorily completed the following exercises: heel on leash and figure eight, heel free, stand for examination, recall, long sit, and long down. C.D.X. means that tests have been passed on all of those just mentioned plus heel free and figure eight, drop on recall, retrieve on flat, retrieve over high jump, broad jump, long sit, and long down. U.D. indicates that the dog has additionally passed tests in scent discrimination (leather article), scent discrimination (metal article), signal exercise, directed retrieve, directed jumping, and group stand for examination. The letters O.T.Ch. are the abbreviation for the only obedience title which precedes rather than follows a dog's name. To gain an obedience trial championship, a dog who already holds a Utility Dog degree must win a total of one hundred points and must win three

Alert little obedience dog, Okatoma's Mr. Cool, C.D.X., "Fonzie" to friends, in the Novice ring at the local obedience trial giving full attention to his handler. Bred, owned, and handled by Patricia Lambert, Hattiesburg, Mississippi.

firsts, under three different judges, in Utility and Open B Classes.

There is also a Tracking Dog title (T.D.) which can be earned at tracking trials. In order to pass the tracking tests the dog must follow the trail of a stranger along a path on which the trail was laid between thirty minutes and two hours previously. Along this track there must be more than two right-angle turns, at least two of which are well out in the open where no fences or other boundaries exist for the guidance of the dog or the handler. The dog

241

This talented long-coated Chihuahua is My Spanish Princess, Canadian and American U.D., owned by Susan Fischer Payne, Suffield, Connecticut. Photo courtesy of Mrs. Ruth Terry, Weston, Connecticut.

wears a harness and is connected to the handler by a lead twenty to forty feet in length. Inconspicuously dropped at the end of the track is an article to be retrieved, usually a glove or wallet, which the dog is expected to locate and the handler to pick up. The letters T.D.X. is the abbreviation for Tracking Dog Excellent, a more difficult version of the Tracking Dog test with a longer track and more turns to be worked through.

SOME LEADING OBEDIENCE CHIHUAHUA "STARS"

Perhaps you are one of those persons who have always felt that Chihuahuas are too small in size to fare well in obedience, in which case you have been sadly mistaken, as I am sure this section will convince you as we examine the successes of some of the noted Chihuahuas who have earned fame in this area.

Take the Brite Star Chihuahuas, for example, who are rapidly becoming a legend in their own time for their owner, Ms. Elizabeth Bickel. This all started with the accident which necessitated retirement from conformation competition for the English importation, Fantasia. She was too beautiful to just sit home, her owner felt, and so obedience work was tried with her. In late 1982, Fantasia added a C.D. to her name, and started her owner on the road to becoming a very famous lady in the world of Chihuahua handler-trainers. During the three years since Fantasia finished, six more C.D. degrees and two C.D.X. degrees had been earned on homebred Brite Star Chihuahuas by mid-1985. Currently the amazing numer of *eight* different Chihuahuas in this kennel are preparing to go for various additional obedience titles, including

High in Trial Winner, Ch. Brite Star Christmas Canis, C.D. practicing the "Retrieve Over High Jump" exercise in preparation for her C.D.X. title. Owned by Ms. Elizabeth Bickel, Kansas City, Missouri.

Bright Star Christmas Dream, C.D.X., doing an Open B broad jump. Ms. Elizabeth Bickel, owner, Kansas City, Missouri.

Utility. And the author ventures to predict that one may well, in time, become an Obedience Trial Champion at the rate things are progressing. Brite Star obedience scores have been consistently in the 190's, usually in the mid to upper range, and these have been consistent placers. Most exciting of all, Brite Star Chihuahuas are holding their own in keenest *all breed* competition. Just look at the accomplishments of litter-mates Champion Bright Star Christmas Canis, C.D., who was the only Chihuahua to receive an all-breed High in Trial in 1984 and one of the only a very few Chihuahuas ever to have gained this honor. She was ranked #1 Obedience Chihuahua for the year 1984, plus the distinction of being among the Top Ten of *all* Obedience Toys. Her brother, Brite Star Christmas Dream, C.D.X., also earned a tie High in Trial, making these two, sister and brother, a unique pair as the only two Chihuahua litter-mates to have accomplished this. Orion selected a nice place to show off his talents, as it was at the huge and prestigious American Kennel Club Centennial Dog Show in November 1984 that he tied for first place in his Novice Class, winning High Scoring Chihuahua over record competition.

In 1985 alone Brite Star put obedience titles on at least four new dogs, all with numerous class placements including many firsts. All are high in both the Delaney and Shuman ratings, and it looks as though Orion will be #1 in the Delaney with Christmas Canis doing likewise in the Shuman.

At Brite Star each new litter is bred with both conformation and obedience aptitude in mind, the goal being a well balanced, physically sound, emotionally adjusted Chihuahua. To her knowledge, Ms. Bickel is the only show breeder to continuously produce Chihuahuas capable of winning high honors in *both* conformation and obedience, a fact in which she justifiably takes tremendous pride.

"Fonzie" taking a jump with ease. This little dog, Okatoma's Mr. Cool, C.D.X., is one of the Top 10 Obedience Chihuahuas for 1984. He did a lot of winning in the Open ring, and is now in training for Utility. Bred, owned, and handled by Patricia Lambert, Hattiesburg, Mississippi.

SOME THEORIES ABOUT CHIHUAHUAS
AND OBEDIENCE

by Madeleine R. Varner, owner of Varner's Choice Chihuahuas.

MRS. VARNER HAD CONSIDERABLE SUCCESS WITH HER DOG IN OBEDIENCE. THUS WE FEEL THAT HER THOUGHTS AND COMMENTS ON WHAT MAKES A DOG SUITABLE FOR THIS TYPE OF WORK SHOULD PROVE INTERESTING TO OUR READERS.

Ch Varner's Fancy Feliciana as a puppy. By Ch. Herron's Feliz Aguinaldo ex Varner's Jenny Me Lo Dijo Adela, C.D. Bred and owned by Madeleine R. Varner, Varner's Choice Chihuahuas, Westville, Florida.

The behavior patterns of a dog are set in motion immediately at the time of birth. I have noted, and charted on our Chihuahuas, the manner in which each litter was born (and sometimes the birth order), feeling that such things as whether a single puppy or multiple puppies, weight of birth, manner of birth (free whelped, difficult, or Caesarean), and even whether the litter was born at the veterinarian's office during office hours or when the hospital was quiet following business hours, each can affect the future obedience pattern of each individual puppy. The pup is further influenced by the attitude of his dam, surroundings and environment in which raised, and type of human contact. The pup will be responding to conditions (stimuli) which are set in motion by both surroundings and environment and by genetic inheritance. Genetics and environment are entwined in a unique manner which does without a doubt affect and determine the final behavior development of the individual pup.

Animal behavior is a result of consequences. Behavior possibly can be changed systematically and even improved. Behavior followed by immediate positive reinforcement such as praise, will affect the behavior displayed by the dog in the future. One must observe and take advantage of the variances in animal behavior

Ch. Varner's Lisa Bonita Milagro, by Ch. Herron's Feliz Aguinaldo ex Varner's Caliente Chispa. Winners Bitch at the 1977 Chihuahua Club of America Specialty in Albany, Georgia. Bred and owned by Madeleine R. Varner.

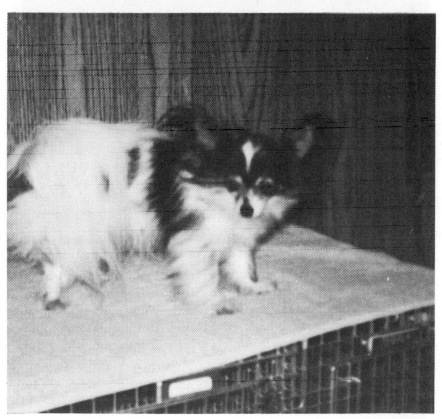

and quickly direct positive reirforcement to *only* the desired responses one wants to imprint into the mind of the dog.

Unwanted behavior does not deserve any verbal comment in the form of human words, but should be addressed by a *sound* that will interrupt the dog's thought pattern and then verbally directed (using only KEY words) toward wanted behavior and *immediately* praised verbally for the correct action. Dogs are very conscious of pitch, phrasing and tone. Dogs interact with each other non-verbally, using such sounds as "Uh-Uh" or "Ah-Ah" means *no*. The "Ah-Ah" *no* is used in communicating to the dog that we are dis-

Varner's Jenny Me Lo Dijo Adela, C.D. working towards her C.D.X. Bred, owned, and trained by Madeleine R. Varner.

Varner's Jenny Me Lo Dijo Adela, C.D., was bred and is owned by Madeleine R. Varner, Westville, Florida.

pleased with his behavior and is used to *stop* the dog from continuing an unwanted action, or moving into an unwanted direction, such as coming at a jump. Other sounds of man are laughter, crying, sobbing, screaming, etc. Man also uses familiar sounds that are non-verbal in communication with his fellow man; an ambulance siren, police siren, car horn, clock chimes, etc. All are sounds that convey a message without the use of words.

Body movements and gestures are another way in which man communicates. They are frowning, smiling, shaking the head for "yes" or "no." Yawning, finger over lips to denote silence are other ways. Man's language, words, is simply a sophisticated verbal communication system of sounds devised to enable humans to interact with each other; but only between persons who can *hear* unless one has studied lip reading, and understands the words being formed with the lips or spoken. Facial expressions and body movements (hands in sign language) are all integral as well as essential elements in communication between humans as well as between man and his dog.

"Huggybear" relaxing in "heel-sit" position during obedience training. Judy Padgug, owner and handler, JP Chihuahuas, Sacramento, California.

Since the dog's language is non-verbal, it interacts not only to sounds, but also by body movements and gestures: strutting, circling, pacing, tail wagging, extending a paw, ears laid back, etc. Once *dependable desired behavior patterns* have been established in the Chihuahua puppy (stopping an unwanted behavior action, coming *quickly* when called, etc.), all future training as well as obedience training will be easier and more enjoyable for both Chihuahua and owner.

Emotional security and reassurance makes for happy Chihuahua pups and grown dogs. Happy fronts and finishes!

Chapter 14

Breeding Your Chihuahua

The first responsibility of any person breeding dogs is to do so with care, forethought, and deliberation. It is inexcusable to breed more litters than you need to carry on your show program or to perpetuate your bloodlines. A responsible breeder should not cause a litter to be born without definite plans for the safe and happy disposition of the puppies.

A responsible dog breeder makes absolutely certain, so far as is humanly possible, that the home to which one of his puppies will go is a good home, one that offers proper care and an enthusiastic owner. To be admired are those breeders who insist on visiting (although doing so is not always feasible) the prospective owners of their puppies to see if they have suitable facilities for keeping a dog, to find out if they understand the responsibility involved, and to make certain if all members of the household are in accord regarding the desirability of owning one. All breeders should carefully check out the credentials of prospective purchasers to be sure that the puppy is being placed in responsible hands.

No breeder ever wants a puppy or grown dog he has raised to wind up in an animal shelter, in an experimental laboratory, or as a victim of a speeding car. While complete control of such a situation may be impossible, it is important to make every effort to turn over dogs to responsible people. When selling a puppy, it is a good idea to do so with the understanding that should it become necessary to place the dog in other hands, the purchaser will first contact you, the breeder. You may want to help in some way, possibly by buying or taking back the dog or placing it elsewhere. It is not fair to sell puppies and then never again give a thought to their welfare. Family problems arise, people may be forced to move where dogs are prohibited, or people just grow bored with a dog and its care. Thus the dog becomes a victim. You, as the dog's breeder, should concern yourself with the welfare of each of your dogs and see to it that the dog remains in good hands.

The final obligation every dog owner shares, be there just one dog or an entire kennel involved, is that of making detailed, explicit plans for the future of these dearly loved animals in the event of the owner's death. Far too many people are apt to procrastinate and leave this very important matter unattended to, feeling that everything will work out or that "someone will see to them." Neither is too likely, at least not to the benefit of the dogs, unless you have done some advance planning which will assure their future well-being.

Life is filled with the unexpected, and even the youngest, healthiest, most robust of us may be the victim of a fatal accident or sudden illness. The fate of your dogs, so entirely in your hands, should never be left to chance. If you have not already done so, please get together with your lawyer and set up a clause in your will specifying what you want done with each of your dogs, to whom they will be entrusted (after first making absolutely certain that the person selected is willing and able to assume the responsibility), and telling the locations of all registration papers, pedigrees, and kennel records. Just think of the possibilities which might happen otherwise! If there is another family member who shares your love of the dogs, that is good and you have less to worry about. But if your heirs are not dog-oriented, they will hardly know how to proceed or how to cope with the dogs themselves, and they may wind up disposing of or caring for your dogs in a manner that would break your heart were you around to know about it.

It is advisable to have in your will specific instructions concerning each of your dogs. A friend, also a dog person who regards his or her own dogs with the same concern and esteem as you do, may agree to take over their care until they can be placed accordingly and will make certain that all will work out as you have planned. This person's name and phone number can be prominently displayed in your van or car and in your wallet. Your lawyer can be made aware of this fact. This can be spelled out in your will. The friend can have a signed check of yours to be used in case of an emergency or accident when you are traveling with the dogs; this check can be used to cover his or her expense to come and take over the care of your dogs should anything happen to make it impossible for you to do so. This is the least any dog owner should do in preparation for the time their dogs suddenly find themselves alone. There have been so many sad cases of dogs unprovided for by their loving owners, left to heirs who couldn't care less and who disposed of them in any way at all to get rid of them, or left to heirs who kept and neglected them under the misguided idea that they were providing them "a fine home with lots of freedom." These misfortunes must be prevented from befalling your own dogs who have meant so much you!

Conscientious breeders feel quite strongly that the only possible reason for producing puppies is the ambition to improve and uphold quality and temperament within the breed—definitely *not* because one hopes to make a quick cash profit on a mediocre litter, which never seems to work out that way in the long run and which accomplishes little beyond perhaps adding to the nation's heartbreaking number of unwanted canines. The only reason ever for breeding a litter is, with conscientious people, a desire to improve the quality of dogs in their own kennel or, as pet owners, to add to the number of dogs they themselves own with a puppy or two from their present favorites. In either case, breeding should not take place unless one definitely has prospective owners for as many puppies as the litter may contain, lest you find yourself with several fast-growing young dogs and no homes in which to place them.

THE BROOD BITCH

Bitches should not be mated earlier than their second season, by which time they should be from fifteen to eighteen months old. Many breeders prefer to wait and finish the championships of their show bitches before breeding them, as pregnancy can be a disaster to a show coat and getting the bitch back in shape again takes time. When you have decided what will be the proper time, start watching at least several months ahead for what you feel would be the perfect mate to best complement your bitch's quality and bloodlines. Subscribe to the magazines which feature your breed exclusively and to some which cover all breeds in order to familiarize yourself with outstanding stud dogs in areas other than your own, for there is no necessity nowadays to limit your choice to a local dog unless you truly like him and feel that he is the most suitable. It is quite usual to ship a bitch to a stud dog a distance away, and this generally works out with no ill effects. The important thing is that you need a stud dog strong in those features where your bitch is weak, a dog whose bloodlines are compatible with hers. Compare the background of both your bitch and the stud dog under consideration, paying particular attention to the quality of the puppies from bitches with backgrounds similar to your bitch's. If the puppies have been of the type and quality you admire, then this dog would seem a sensible choice for yours, too.

Stud fees may be a few hundred dollars, sometimes even more under special situations for a particularly successful sire. It is money well spent, however. *Do not* ever breed to a dog because he is less expensive than the others unless you honestly believe that he can sire the kind of puppies who will be a credit to your kennel and your breed.

Contacting the owners of the stud dogs you find interesting will bring you pedigrees and pictures which you can then study in relation to your bitch's pedigree and conformation. Discuss your plans with other breeders who are knowledgeable (including the one who bred your own bitch). You may not always receive an entirely unbiased opinion (particularly if the person giving it also has an available stud dog), but one learns by discussion so listen to what they say, consider their opinions, and then you may be better qualified to form your own opinion.

As soon as you have made a choice, phone the owner of the stud dog you wish to use to find out if this will be agreeable. You will be asked about the bitch's health, soundness, temperament, and freedom from serious faults. A copy of her pedigree may be requested, as might a picture of her. A discussion of her background over the telephone may be sufficient to assure the stud's owner that she is suitable for the stud dog and that she is of type, breeding, and quality herself, capable of producing the kind of puppies for which the stud is noted. The owner of a top-quality stud is often extremely selective in the bitches permitted to be bred to his dog, in an effort to keep the standard of his puppies high. The owner of a stud dog may require that the bitch be tested for brucellosis, which should be attended to not more than a month previous to the breeding.

Check out which airport will be most convenient for the person meeting and returning the bitch, if she is to be shipped, and also what airlines use that airport. You will find that the airlines are also apt to have special requirements concerning acceptance of animals for shipping. These include weather limitations and types of crates which are acceptable. The weather limits have to do with extreme heat and extreme cold at the point of destination, as some airlines will not fly dogs into temperatures above or below certain levels, fearing for their safety. The crate problem is a simple one, since, if your own crate is not suitable, most of the airlines have specially designed crates available for purchase at a fair and moderate price. It is a good plan to purchase one of these if you intend to be shipping dogs with any sort of frequency. They are made of fiberglass and are the safest type to use for shipping.

Normally you must notify the airline several days in advance to make a reservation, as they are able to accommodate only a certain number of dogs on each flight. Plan on shipping the bitch on about her eighth or ninth day of season, but be careful to avoid shipping her on a weekend when schedules often vary and freight offices are apt to be closed. Whenever you can, ship your bitch on a direct flight. Changing planes always carries a certain amount of risk of a dog being overlooked or wrongly routed at the middle stop, so avoid this danger if at all possible. The bitch must be accompanied by a health certificate which you must obtain from your veterinarian before taking her to the airport. Usually it will be necessary to have the bitch at the airport about two hours prior to flight time. Before finalizing arrangements, find out from the stud's owner at what time of day it will be most convenient to have the bitch picked up promptly upon arrival.

It is simpler if you can bring the bitch to the stud dog yourself. Some people feel that the trauma of the flight may cause the bitch to not conceive; and, of course, undeniably there is a slight risk

Glindale Pee Wee Power and Glindale's Tru Blu Sam showing off their beautiful head quality. Owned by Linda M. Glenn, Glindale Chihuahuas, Harrington Park, New Jersey. Photo by Herbert Horowitz.

in shipping which can be avoided if you are able to drive the bitch to her destination. Be sure to leave yourself sufficient time to assure your arrival at the right time for her for breeding (normally the tenth to fourteenth day following the first signs of color); and remember that if you want the bitch bred twice, you should allow a day to elapse between the two matings. Do not expect the stud's owner to house you while you are there. Locate a nearby motel that takes dogs and make that your headquarters.

Just prior to the time your bitch is due in season, you should take her to visit your veterinarian. She should be checked for worms and should receive all the booster shots for which she is due plus one for parvovirus, unless she has had the latter shot fairly recently. The brucellosis test can also be done then, and the health certificate can be obtained for shipping if she is to travel by air. Should the bitch be at all overweight, now is the time to get the surplus off. She should be in good condition, neither underweight nor overweight, at the time of breeding.

The moment you notice the swelling of the vulva, for which you should be checking daily as the time for her season approaches, and the appearance of color, immediately contact the stud's owner and settle on the day for shipping or make the appointment for your arrival with the bitch for breeding. If you are shipping the

Call's Plaudits for Pittipat at six and a half weeks. Bred and owned by Call's Chihuahuas, Chester P. and Annie D. Carr, Kaysville, Utah.

Ch. Call's Little Buddy Buckshot with one of his Best in Show rosettes from 1981. Note the quality of this stunning little dog! Owner-handled by Annie D. Call, Kaysville, Utah.

bitch, the stud fee check should be mailed immediately, leaving ample time for it to have been received when the bitch arrives and the mating takes place. Be sure to call the airline, making her reservation at that time, too.

Do not feed the bitch within a few hours before shipping her. Be certain that she has had a drink of water and been well exercised before closing her in the crate. Several layers of newspapers, topped with some shredded newspaper, make a good bed and can be discarded when she arrives at her destination; these can be replaced with fresh newspapers for her return home. Remember that the bitch should be brought to the airport about two hours before flight time, as sometimes the airlines refuse to accept late arrivals.

If you are taking your bitch by car, be certain that you will arrive at a reasonable time of day. Do not appear late in the evening. If your arrival in town is not until late, get a good night's sleep at your motel and contact the stud's owner first thing in the morning. If possible, leave children and relatives at home, as they will only be in the way and perhaps unwelcome by the stud's owner. Most stud dog owners prefer not to have any unnecessary people on hand during the actual mating.

After the breeding has taken place, if you wish to sit and visit for awhile and the stud's owner has the time, return the bitch to her crate in your car (first ascertaining, of course, that the temperature is comfortable for her and that there is proper ventilation). She should not be permitted to urinate for at least one hour following the breeding. This is the time when you attend to the business part of the transaction. Pay the stud fee, upon which you should receive your breeding certificate and, if you do not already have it, a copy of the stud dog's pedigree. The owner of the stud dog does not sign or furnish a litter registration application until the puppies have been born.

Upon your return home, you can settle down and plan in happy anticipation a wonderful litter of puppies. A word of caution! Remember that although she has been bred, your bitch is still an interesting target for all male dogs, so guard her carefully for the next week or until you are absolutely certain that her season has entirely ended. This would be no time to have any unfortunate incident with another dog.

THE STUD DOG

Choosing the best stud dog to complement your bitch is often very difficult. The two principal factors to be considered should be the stud's conformation and his pedigree. Conformation is fairly obvious; you want a dog that is typical of the breed in the words of the Standard of perfection. Understanding pedigrees is a bit more subtle since the pedigree lists the ancestry of the dog and involves individuals and bloodlines with which you may not be entirely familiar.

To a novice in the breed, the correct interpretation of a pedigree may at first be difficult to grasp. Study the pictures and text of this book and you will find many names of important bloodlines and members of the breed. Also make an effort to discuss the various dogs behind the proposed stud with some of the more experienced breeders, starting with the breeder of your own bitch. Frequently these folks will be familiar with many of the dogs in question, will be able to offer opinions of them, and may have access to additional pictures which you would benefit by seeing. It is very important that the stud's pedigree be harmonious with that of the bitch you plan on breeding to him. Do not rush out and breed to the latest winner with no thought of whether or not he can produce true quality. By no means are all great show dogs great producers. It is the producing record of the dog in question, and the dogs and bitches from which he has come, that should be the basis on which you make your choice.

Breeding dogs is never a money-making operation. By the time you pay a stud fee, care for the bitch during pregnancy, whelp the litter, and rear the puppies through their early shots, worming, and so on, you will be fortunate to break even financially once the puppies have been sold. Your chances of doing this are greater if you are breeding for a show-quality litter which will bring you higher prices, as the pups are sold as show prospects. Therefore, your wisest investment is to use the best dog available for your bitch regardless of the cost; then you should wind up with more valuable puppies. Remember that it is equally costly to raise mediocre puppies as it is top ones, and your chances of financial return are better on the latter. Breeding to the most excellent, most suitable stud dog you can find is the only sensible thing to do, and it is poor economy to quibble over the amount you are paying in a stud fee.

It will be your decision as to which course you follow when you breed your bitch, as there are three options: linebreeding, inbreeding, and outcrossing. Each of these methods has its supporters and its detractors! Linebreeding is breeding a bitch to a dog belonging originally to the same canine family, being descended from the same ancestors, such as half brother to half sister, grandsire to granddaughter, niece to uncle (and vice-versa) or cousin to cousin. Inbreeding is breeding father to daughter, mother to son, or full brother to sister. Outcross breeding is breeding a dog and a bitch with no or only a few mutual ancestors.

Linebreeding is probably the safest course, and the one most likely to bring results, for the novice breeder. The more sophisticated inbreeding should be left to the experienced, longtime breeders who thoroughly know and understand the risks and the possibilities involved with a particular line. It is usually done in an effort to intensify some ideal feature in that strain. Outcrossing

A lovely Long Coat from the early 1960s. Ch. Bell's Tinker Bell winning Best of Variety under the author at the Chihuahua Club of Greater New York Specialty in 1960. Owner-handled by Mrs. Dorothy Bell who bred a number of outstanding Long Coats around this period.

is the reverse of inbreeding, an effort to introduce improvement in a specific feature needing correction, such as a shorter back, better movement, more correct head or coat, and so on.

It is the serious breeder's ambition to develop a strain or bloodline of their own, one strong in qualities for which their dogs will become distinguished. However, it must be realized that this will involve time, patience, and at least several generations before the achievement can be claimed. The safest way to embark on this plan, as previously mentioned, is by the selection and breeding of one or two bitches, the best you can buy and from top-producing kennels. In the beginning you do *not* really have to own a stud dog. In the long run it is less expensive and sounder judgement to pay a stud fee when you are ready to breed a bitch than to purchase a stud dog and feed him all year; a stud dog does not win any popularity contests with owners of bitches to be bred until he becomes a champion, has been successfully Specialed for a while, and has been at least moderately advertised, all of which adds up to quite a healthy expenditure.

The wisest course for the inexperienced breeder just starting out in dogs is to keep the best bitch puppy from the first several litters. After that you may wish to consider keeping your own stud dog, if there has been a particularly handsome male in one of your litters that you feel has great potential or if you know where there is one available that you are interested in, with the feeling that he would work in nicely with the breeding program on which you have embarked. By this time, with several litters already born, your eye should have developed to a point enabling you to make a wise choice, either from one of your own litters or from among dogs you have seen that appear suitable.

The greatest care should be taken in the selection of your own stud dog. He must be of true type and highest quality as he may be responsible for siring many puppies each year, and he should come from a line of excellent dogs on both sides of his pedigree which themselves are, and which are descended from, successful producers. This dog should have no glaring faults in conformation; he should be of such quality that he can hold his own in keenest competition within his breed. He should be in good health, be virile and be a keen stud dog, a proven sire able to transmit his correct qualities to his puppies. Need one say that such a dog will be enormously expensive unless you have the good fortune to produce him in one of your own litters? To buy and use a lesser stud dog, however, is downgrading your breeding program unnecessarily since there are so many dogs fitting the description of a fine stud whose services can be used on payment of a stud fee.

You should *never* breed to an unsound dog or one with any serious disqualifying faults according to the breed's standard. Not all champions by any means pass along their best features; and by the same token, occasionally you will find a great one who can pass along his best features but never gained his championship title due to some unusual circumstances. The information you need about a stud dog is what type of puppies he has produced, and with what bloodlines, and whether or not he possesses the bloodlines and attributes considered characteristic of the best in your breed.

If you go out to buy a stud. dog, obviously he will not be a puppy, but rather a fully mature and proven male with as many of the best attributes as possible. True, he will be an expensive investment, but if you choose and make his selection with care and forethought, he may well prove to be one of the best investments you have ever made.

Of course, the most exciting of all is when a young male you have decided to keep from one of your litters, due to his tremendous show potential, turns out to be a stud dog such as we have described. In this case he should be managed with care, for he is a valuable property that can contribute inestimably to this breed as a whole and to your own kennel specifically.

Do not permit your stud dog to be used until he is about a year old, and even then he should be bred to a mature, proven matron accustomed to breeding who will make his first experience pleasant and easy. A young dog can be put off forever by a maiden bitch who fights and resists his advances. Never allow this to happen. Always start a stud dog out with a bitch who is mature, has been bred previously, and is of even temperament. The first breeding should be performed in quiet surroundings with only you and one other person to hold the bitch. Do not make it a circus, as the experience will determine the dog's outlook about future stud work. If he does not enjoy the first experience or associ-

Chihuahua puppies at play, quite unconcerned by the cat outside their fence. Dorothy Pratt, owner, Pratt's Chihuahuas, Lakeland, Florida.

ates it with any unpleasantness, you may well have a problem in the future.

Your young stud must permit help with the breeding, as later there will be bitches who will not be cooperative. If right from the beginning you are there helping him and praising him, whether or not your assistance is actually needed, he will expect and accept this as a matter of course when a difficult bitch comes along.

Things to have handy before introducing your dog and the bitch are K-Y jelly (the only lubricant which should be used) and a length of gauze with which to muzzle the bitch should it be necessary to keep her from biting you or the dog. Some bitches put up a fight; others are calm. It is best to be prepared.

264

At the time of the breeding, the stud fee comes due, and it is expected that it will be paid promptly. Normally a return service is offered in case the bitch misses or fails to produce one live puppy. Conditions of the service are what the stud dog's owner makes them, and there are no standard rules covering this. The stud fee is paid for the act, not the result. If the bitch fails to conceive, it is customary for the owner to offer a free return service; but this is a courtesy and not to be considered a right, particularly in the case of a proven stud who is siring consistently and whose fault the failure obviously is *not*. Stud dog owners are always anxious to see their clients get good value and to have, in the ring, winning young stock by their dog; therefore, very few refuse to mate the second time. It is wise, however, for both parties to have the terms of the transaction clearly understood at the time of the breeding.

Tiny Mite's DeJonge's Taffy (*center*), with some of the puppies. Bred and owned by Tiny Mite Chihuahuas, Robert L. DeJonge, Zeeland, Michigan.

If the return service has been provided and the bitch has missed a second time, that is considered to be the end of the matter and the owner would be expected to pay a further fee if it is felt that the bitch should be given a third chance with the stud dog. The management of a stud dog and his visiting bitches is quite a task, and a stud fee has usually been well earned when one service has been achieved, let alone by repeated visits from the same bitch.

The accepted litter is one live puppy. It is wise to have printed a breeding certificate which the owner of the stud dog and the owner of the bitch both sign. This should list in detail the conditions of the breeding as well as the dates of the mating.

H and J's Cocoa Princess as a newborn, dwarfed by a child's hand. H and J Kennels, Jack and Hilda Phariss, Bryan Texas.

Upon occasion, arrangements other than a stud fee in cash are made for a breeding, such as the owner of the stud taking a pick-of-the-litter puppy in lieu of money. This should be clearly specified on the breeding certificate along with the terms of the age at which the stud's owner will select the puppy, whether it is to be a specific sex, or whether it is to be the pick of the entire litter.

The price of a stud fee varies according to circumstances. Usually, to prove a young stud dog, his owner will allow the first breeding to be quite inexpensive. Then, once a bitch has become pregnant by him, he becomes a "proven stud" and the fee rises accordingly for bitches that follow. The sire of championship quality puppies will bring a stud fee of at least the purchase price of one show puppy as the accepted "rule-of-thumb." Until at least one champion by your stud dog has finished, the fee will remain equal to the price of one pet puppy. When his list of champions starts to grow, so does the amount of the stud fee. For a top-producing sire of champions, the stud fee will rise accordingly.

Almost invariably it is the bitch who comes to the stud dog for the breeding. Immediately upon having selected the stud dog you wish to use, discuss the possibility with the owner of that dog. It is the stud dog owner's prerogative to refuse to breed any bitch deemed unsuitable for this dog. Stud fee and method of payment should be stated at this time and a decision reached on whether it is to be a full cash transaction at the time of the mating or a pick-of-the-litter puppy, usually at eight weeks of age.

If the owner of the stud dog must travel to an airport to meet the bitch and ship her for the flight home, an additional charge will be made for time, tolls, and gasoline based on the stud owner's proximity to the airport. The stud fee includes board for the day on the bitch's arrival through two days for breeding, with a day in between. If it is necessary that the bitch remain longer, it is very likely that additional board will be charged at the normal per-day rate for the breed.

Be sure to advise the stud's owner as soon as you know that your bitch is in season so that the stud dog will be available. This is especially important because if he is a dog being shown, he and his owner may be unavailable, owing to the dog's absence from home.

Call's Penny
Princess with her
puppies. Chester P.
and Annie D. Call,
owners, Kaysville,
Utah.

As the owner of a stud dog being offered to the public, it is essential that you have proper facilities for the care of visiting bitches. Nothing can be worse than a bitch being insecurely housed and slipping out to become lost or bred by the wrong dog. If you are taking people's valued bitches into your kennel or home, it is imperative that you provide them with comfortable, secure housing and good care while they are your responsibility.

There is no dog more valuable than the proven sire of champions, Group winners, and Best in Show dogs. Once you have such an animal, guard his reputation well and do *not* permit him to be bred to just any bitch that comes along. It takes two to make the puppies; even the most dominant stud cannot do it all himself, so never permit him to breed a bitch you consider unworthy. Remember that when the puppies arrive, it will be your stud dog who will be blamed for any lack of quality, while the bitch's shortcomings will be quickly and conveniently overlooked.

Going into the actual management of the mating is a bit superfluous here. If you have had previous experience in breeding a dog and bitch, you will know how the mating is done. If you do not have such experience, you should not attempt to follow directions given in a book but should have a veterinarian, breeder friend, or handler there to help you with the first few times. You do not turn the dog and bitch loose together and await developments, as too many things can go wrong and you may altogether miss getting the bitch bred. Someone should hold the dog and the bitch (one person each) until the "tie" is made and these two people should stay with them during the entire act.

If you get a complete tie, probably only the one mating is absolutely necessary. However, especially with a maiden bitch or one that has come a long distance for this breeding, a follow-up with a second breeding is preferred, leaving one day in between the two matings. In this way there will be little or no chance of the bitch missing.

Once the tie has been completed and the dogs release, be certain that the male's penis goes completely back within its sheath. He should be allowed a drink of water and a short walk, and then he should be put into his crate or somewhere alone where he can settle down. Do not allow him to be with other dogs for a while as they will notice the odor of the bitch on him, and, particularly

Grindale's Little Bit of Sampsen snapped informally in Bermuda, a lovely candid shot of an excellent Chihuahua. Linda M. Glenn, owner, Harrington Park, New Jersey.

with other males present, he may become involved in a fight.

PREGNANCY, WHELPING, AND THE LITTER

Once the bitch has been bred and is back at home, remember to keep an ever watchful eye that no other males get to her until at least the twenty-second day of her season has passed. Until then, it will still be possible for an unwanted breeding to take place, which at this point would be catastrophic. Remember that she actually can have two separate litters by two different dogs, so take care.

In other ways, she should be treated normally. Controlled exercise is good and necessary for the bitch throughout her pregnancy, tapering it off to just several short walks daily, preferably on lead, as she reaches her seventh week. As her time grows close, be careful about her jumping or playing too roughly.

The theory that a bitch should be overstuffed with food when pregnant is a poor one. A fat bitch is never an easy whelper, so the overfeeding you consider good for her may well turn out to be a hindrance later on. During the first few weeks of pregnancy, your bitch should be fed her normal diet. At four to five weeks along, calcium should be added to her food. At seven weeks her food may be increased if she seems to crave more than she is getting, and a meal of canned milk (mixed with an equal amount of water) should be introduced. If she is fed just once a day, add another meal rather than overload her with too much at one time. If twice a day is her schedule, then a bit more food can be added to each feeding.

A week before the pups are due, your bitch should be introduced to her whelping box so that she will be accustomed to it and feel at home there when the puppies arrive. She should be encouraged to sleep there but permitted to come and go as she wishes. The box should be roomy enough for her to lie down and stretch out in but not too large, lest the pups have more room than is needed in which to roam and possibly get chilled by going too far away from their mother. Be sure that the box has a "pig rail"; this will prevent the puppies from being crushed against the sides. The room in which the box is placed, either in your home or in the kennel, should be kept at about 70 degrees Fahrenheit. In winter it may be necessary to have an infrared lamp over the whelping box, in which case be careful not to place it too low or close to the puppies.

Newspapers will become a very important commodity, so start collecting them well in advance to have a big pile handy for the whelping box. With a litter of puppies, one never seems to have papers enough, so the higher pile to start with, the better off you will be. Other necessities for whelping time are clean, soft turkish towels, scissors, and a bottle of alcohol.

You will know that her time is very near when your bitch becomes restless, wandering in and out of her box and out of the room. She may refuse food, and at that point her temperature will start to drop. She will dig at and tear up the newspapers in her box, shiver, and generally look uncomfortable. Only you should be with your bitch at this time. She does not need spectators; and several people hanging over her, even though they may be family members whom she knows, may upset her to the point where she may harm the puppies. You should remain nearby, quietly watching, not fussing or hovering; speak calmly and frequently to her to instill confidence. Eventually she will settle down in her box and begin panting; contractions will follow. Soon thereafter a puppy will start to emerge, sliding out with the contractions. The mother immediately should open the sac, sever the cord with her teeth, and then clean up the puppy. She will also eat the placenta, which you should permit. Once the puppy is cleaned, it should be placed next to the bitch unless she is showing signs of having the next one immediately. Almost at once the puppy will start looking for a nipple on which to nurse, and you should ascertain that it is able to latch on successfully.

If the puppy is a breech (*i.e.*, born feet first), you must watch carefully for it to be completely delivered as quickly as possible and for the sac to be removed quickly so that the puppy does not drown. Sometimes even a normally positioned birth will seem extremely slow in coming. Should this occur, you might take a clean towel, and as the bitch contracts, pull the puppy out, doing so gently and with utmost care. If, once the puppy is delivered, it shows little signs of life, take a rough turkish towel and massage the puppy's chest by rubbing quite briskly back and forth. Continue this for about fifteen minutes, and be sure that the mouth is free of liquid. It may be necessary to try mouth-to-mouth breath-

Patricia Pittore is the breeder-owner of this beautiful litter of seven Chihuahua puppies, the largest litter she has had in which all puppies reached maturity. We think that this is one of the nicest "nursing mother" pictures we have seen! Pittore's Pollyanna, Pittore's Chihuahuas, Goshen, Massachusetts. Photo dated September 1972.

ing, which is begun by pressing the puppy's jaws open and, using a finger, depressing the tongue which may be stuck to the roof of the mouth. Then place your mouth against the puppy's and blow hard down the puppy's throat. Rub the puppy's chest with the towel again and try artificial respiration, pressing the sides of the chest together slowly and rhythmically—in and out, in and out. Keep trying one method or the other for at least twenty minutes before giving up. You may be rewarded with a live puppy who otherwise would not have made it.

If you are successful in bringing the puppy around, do not immediately put it back with the mother as it should be kept extra warm. Put it in a cardboard box on an electric heating pad or, if it is the time of year when your heat is running, near a radiator or near the fireplace or stove. As soon as the rest of the litter has been born, it then can join the others.

An hour or more may elapse between puppies, which is fine so long as the bitch seems comfortable and is neither straining nor contracting. She should not be permitted to remain unassisted for more than an hour if she does continue to contract. This is when you should get her to your veterinarian, whom you should already have alerted to the possibility of a problem existing. He should examine her and perhaps give her a shot of Pituitrin. In some cases the veterinarian may find that a Caesarean section is necessary due to a puppy being lodged in a manner making normal delivery impossible. Sometimes this is caused by an abnormally large puppy, or it may just be that the puppy is simply turned in the wrong position. If the bitch does require a Caesarean section, the puppies already born must be kept warm in their cardboard box with a heating pad under the box.

Once the section is done, get the bitch and the puppies home. Do not attempt to put the puppies in with the bitch until she has regained consciousness, as she may unknowingly hurt them. But do get them back to her as soon as possible for them to start nursing.

Should the mother lack milk at this time, the puppies must be fed by hand, kept very warm, and held onto the mother's teats several times a day in order to stimulate and encourage the secretion of milk, which should start shortly.

Assuming that there has been no problem and that the bitch has whelped naturally, you should insist that she go out to exercise, staying just long enough to make herself comfortable. She can be offered a bowl of milk and a biscuit, but then she should settle down with her family. Freshen the whelping box for her with newspapers while she is taking this respite so that she and the puppies will have a clean bed.

Unless some problem arises, there is little you must do for the puppies until they become three to four weeks old. Keep the box clean and supplied with fresh newspapers the first few days, but then turkish towels should be tacked down to the bottom of the box so that the puppies will have traction as they move about.

If the bitch has difficulties with her milk supply, or if you should be so unfortunate as to lose her, then you must be prepared to either hand-feed or tube-feed the puppies if they are to survive. Tube-feeding is so much faster and easier. If the bitch is available, it is best that she continues to clean and care for the puppies in the normal manner, excepting for the food supplements you will provide. If it is impossible for her to do this, then after every feeding you must gently rub each puppy's abdomen with wet cotton to make it urinate, and the rectum should be gently rubbed to open the bowels.

Newborn puppies must be fed every three to four hours around the clock. The puppies must be kept warm during this time. Have your veterinarian teach you how to tube-feed. You will find that it is really quite simple.

After a normal whelping, the bitch will require additional food to enable her to produce sufficient milk. In addition to being fed twice daily, she should be given some canned milk several times each day.

When the puppies are two weeks old, their nails should be clipped, as they are needle sharp at this age and can hurt or damage the mother's teats and stomach as the pups hold on to nurse.

Between three and four weeks of age, the puppies should begin to be weaned. Scraped beef (prepared by scraping it off slices of beef with a spoon so that none of the gristle is included) may be offered in very small quantities a couple of times daily for the first few days. Then by the third day you can mix puppy chow with warm water as directed on the package, offering it four times

Ch. Mignon's John, owner-handled by Mignon Murray, winning Best Smooth Coat Chihuahua at the Progressive Dog Club in 1974.

daily. By now the mother should be kept away from the puppies and out of the box for several hours at a time so that when they have reached five weeks of age she is left in with them only overnight. By the time the puppies are six weeks old, they should be entirely weaned and receiving only occasional visits from their mother.

Most veterinarians recommend a temporary DHL (distemper, hepatitis, leptospirosis) shot when the puppies are six weeks of age. This remains effective for about two weeks. Then at eight weeks of age, the puppies should receive the series of permanent shots for DHL protection. It is also a good idea to discuss with your vet the advisability of having your puppies inoculated against the dreaded parvovirus at the same time. Each time the pups go to the vet for shots, you should bring stool samples so that they can be examined for worms. Worms go through various stages of development and may be present in a stool sample even though the sample does not test positive in every checkup. So do not neglect to keep careful watch on this.

The puppies should be fed four times daily until they are three months old. Then you can cut back to three feedings daily. By the time the puppies are six months of age, two meals daily are sufficient. Some people feed their dogs twice daily throughout their lifetime; others go to one meal daily when the puppy becomes one year of age.

The ideal age for puppies to go to their new homes is between eight and twelve weeks, although some puppies successfully adjust to a new home when they are six weeks old. Be sure that they go to their new owners accompanied by a description of the diet you've been feeding them and a schedule of the shots they have already received and those they still need. These should be included with the registration application and a copy of the pedigree.

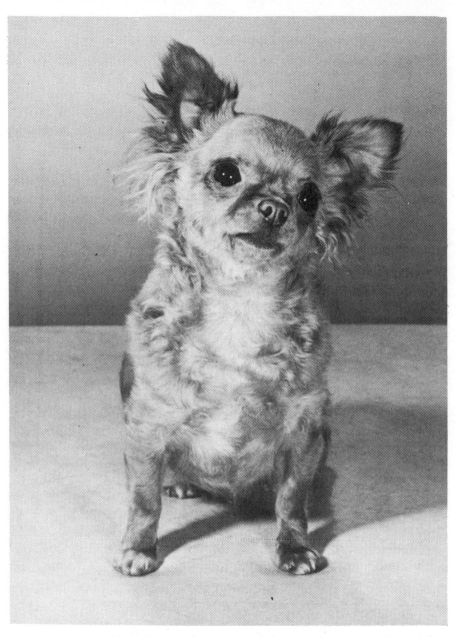

Ch. Terrymont Sweet Cream Taffy, C.D., pictured as a puppy, was bred by Mr. and Mrs. Herbert Terry, Weston, Connecticut, and is owned by Marcia Greenburg, Springfield, Massachusetts. This lovely long-coated bitch of the 1960s gained her obedience degree in three straight shows and her championship title with four majors.

Chapter 15

Traveling with Your Chihuahua

When you travel with your dog, to shows or on vacation or wherever, remember that everyone does not share your enthusiasm or love for dogs and that those who do not, strange creatures though they seem to us, have their rights, too. These rights, on which your should not encroach, include not being disturbed, annoyed, or made uncomfortable by the presence and behavior of other people's pets. Your dog should be kept on lead in public places and should recognize and promptly obey the commands "Down," "Come," "Sit," and "Stay."

Take along his crate if you are going any distance with your dog. And keep him in it when riding in the car. A crated dog has a far better chance of escaping injury than one riding loose in the car, should an accident occur or an emergency arise. If you do permit your dog to ride loose, never allow him to hang out a window, ears blowing in the breeze. An injury to his eyes could occur in this manner. He could also become overly excited by something he sees and jump out, or he could lose his balance and fall out.

If you are staying at a hotel or motel with your dog, exercise him somewhere other than in the flower beds and parking lot of the property. People walking to and from their cars really are not thrilled at "stepping in something" left by your dog. Should an accident occur, pick it up with a tissue or paper towel and deposit it in a proper receptacle; do not just walk off leaving it to remain there. Usually there are grassy areas on the sides of and behind motels where dogs can be exercised. Use them rather than the more conspicuous, usually carefully tended, front areas or those close to the rooms. If you are becoming a dog show enthusiast, you will eventually need an exercise pen to take with you to the show. Exercise pens are ideal to use when staying at motels, too, as they permit you to limit the dog's roaming space and to pick up after him more easily.

Never leave your dog unattended in the room of a motel unless you are absolutely, positively certain that he will stay there quietly and not damage or destroy anything. You do not want a long list of complaints from irate guests, caused by the annoying barking

Ch. Tiny Mite's Gideon winning a Toy Group placement at Battle Creek in 1980. Owned by Robert L. DeJonge, Tiny Mite Chihuahuas, Zeeland, Michigan.

Ch. Komo's Too Sweet Sue Subaru finishes her title with Best of Winners at the Atlanta Chihuahua Club Specialty, April 15, 1985, where she gained her final five-point major. Bred, owned, and handled by Katherine J. Hood, Komo's Chihuahuas, Altamont, Illinois.

or whining of a lonesome dog in strange surroundings or an over-zealous watch dog barking furiously each time a footstep passes the door or he hears a sound from an adjoining room. And you certainly do not want to return to torn curtains or bedspreads, soiled rugs, or other embarrassing evidence of the fact that your dog is not really house-reliable after all.

If yours is a dog accustomed to traveling with you and you are positive that his behavior will be acceptable when left alone, that is fine. But if the slightest uncertainty exists, the wise course is to leave him in the car while you go to dinner or elsewhere; then bring him into the room when you are ready to retire for the night.

When you travel with a dog, it is often simpler to take along from home the food and water he will need rather than to buy food and look for water while you travel. In this way he will have the rations to which he is accustomed and which you know agree with him, and there will be no fear of problems due to different drinking water. Feeding on the road is quite easy now, at least for short trips, with all the splendid dry prepared foods and high-quality canned meats available. A variety of lightweight, refillable water containers can be bought at many types of stores.

Be careful always to leave sufficient openings to ventilate your car when the dog will be alone in it. Remember that during the summer, the rays of the sun can make an inferno of a closed car within only a few minutes, so leave enough window space open to provide air circulation. Again, if your dog is in a crate, this can be done quite safely. The fact that you have left the car in a shady spot is not always a guarantee that you will find conditions the same when you return. Don't forget that the position of the sun changes in a matter of minutes, and the car you left nicely shaded half an hour ago can be getting full sunlight far more quickly than you may realize. So, if you leave a dog in the car, make sure there is sufficient ventilation and check back frequently to ascertain that all is well.

If you are going to another country, you will need a health certificate from your veterinarian for each dog you are taking with you, certifying that each has had rabies shots within the required time preceding your visit.

Index

V

Veterans Class, 227
Veterinarian, 202

W

Western Specialty Clubs Association,
    18
Whelping, 277
Will O'Wisp, 72, 73
Winners Bitch, 224
Winners Class, 221
Winners Dog, 224
Wisherwood, 80
Worms, 277

Index of People

A

Alford, Clara, 21, 23, 45, 62, 76
Allen, Dr. C.L., 18
Alonso, Mr., 107
Anspach, Peggy, 16
Attas, Mrs. Mike, 62, 76
Ayres, Roy, 119

B

Balealb, Cindy, 134, 135
Beam, Maxine, 151
Bedford, Mrs. R.A., 16, 24
Bell, Mrs. Dorothy, 260
Bickel, Ms. Elizabeth, 28, 30, 102,
    103, 110, 114, 123, 147, 142, 143,
    244, 245
Billings, Michelle, 73, 119
Bohrer, Betty, 119
Bradley, Paula, 73
Brearley, Joan, 8
Bridges, Shirley/Robert, 88
Briggs, Mr. & Mrs. Newman K., 18
Brookins, Bonnie, 73
Brown, Thelma, 126
Browne, Kathleen, 110
Browne, Mrs. Debbie, 139, 147, 169

C

Call, Chester P./Annie D., 3, 31, 33,
    106, 107, 118, 131, 134, 258, 268
Callaghan, Mr. & Mrs. H.M., 166,
    167
Carr, Chester P./Annie D., 257
Carsello, Nadine, 18
Caviness, Robert, 33
Chamberlain, Jordan, 66
Clark, Anne Rogers, 139
Clark, Rose, 17
Clay, Mr. R.J., 94
Cohen, Merrill, 66
Cross-Stern, P., 94
Crouse, Mamie, 218
Currie, Mr. J., 94
Currie, Mrs. B., 94

D

DeJonge, Helen, 99
DeJonge, Robert L., 10, 69, 72, 119,
    135, 143, 154, 280
DeJonges, Robert L., 10
Delaney, Darwin/Tanya, 32, 35, 44,
    49, 65, 106, 119, 131, 151
Diaz, Michael, 39, 119, 217
Dickerson, Dick, 126
Dickerson, Pat, 59
Dobb, Alice, 17
Donnell, Mrs. Henrietta Proctor
    (later Reilly), 18, 19
Duncan, J.J., 45,

E

Eagen, Jo Ann, 130
Edwards, H.H., 17
Edwards, Sandra Nelles, 80

F

Faigel, Joe, 47, 139
Febles, Silvina, 18, 24
Field, Dr. William, 103
Field, Dr. William, Jr., 73
Fields, Mr., 57